Author Note

Mark attended Stratfo
Forest Gate, East Lond
main achievements we
mostly unsuccessfully - to be the class joker. As one very
astute teacher once pointed out in his end of year report:

*'Mark spends an inordinate amount of time trying to be the
class clown however there is one fatal flaw in this plan; he's
not very funny'*

Undeterred by this withering assessment, Mark
continued generally arse-ing around, being an idiot and
relying on his foot speed to get him out of various tricky
situations and no-one was more surprised than Mark
(...actually his teachers might have been...) when he left
school with 6 'O'levels. On leaving in 1976, he spent 10
years as a jeweller in Hatton Garden, London, before
going into the sales industry in 1986; where he stayed
until moving to France. Throughout all of this time, his
love for writing, languages and accents remained and,
after moving to France in 2004 and having been told on
numerous occasions that some of the stories should be
written down, the seed and idea of a book was sewn in
his mind. Married to Trudy and father to two cocker
spaniels, they all live in France now where the
adventures are still racking up on a daily basis...

Prologue

Having been raised in the south east of England and having experienced a certain number of highs and lows in my life - I wasn't the 1997 Burnham-on-Crouch over 35s All Comers freestyle Pilates champion for nothing, although this euphoria was soon tempered by the fact that I once knelt on *TWO* Subbuteo players in the same match - my affinity to France was non-existent. My only experience of anything to do with France was when my French teacher got arrested whilst on holiday there.

It wasn't until I got married to the fragrant Trudy, and we holidayed within France that our love for France grew and we came up with a plan to maybe, just maybe, spend more time there in the future. Notwithstanding the fact that I had pretty much annoyed everyone I'd come across in England, I decided I would turn my attention to the French. Trudy had always harboured a desire to run a B&B in France and this story tells how, through adversity, tragedy, and quite a lot of fun, that dream became a reality. I have tried to give you, dear, solitary, reader, an insight into what life in rural France was like and inject some humour into the situations we found ourselves in. To everyone who joined us in the Chambres d'hotes and who therefore made the stories and this book possible, I can only thank you. Some of the names have been changed to protect the innocent, others have been changed because frankly I can't remember your real ones...apologies.

Whoever and wherever you are, absolutely no offence is meant or should be taken; after all, we owe it all to you…

Thank you.

For Trudy x

…and they said it would be boring…

Contents:

Chapter 1 - The Voyage

There is a famous old Chinese proverb by Confucius. It states that '*Even a journey of a thousand miles begins with a single step*' The proverb is actually '*A journey of a thousand li starts beneath one's feet*'....and it's not by Confucius. It was written by Laozi who was instrumental in writing the original text in the 6th century which outlines Taoism. That said, Chairman Mao (before he was Chairman of the People's Party and just worked in Goods In) ***did*** state that "...*you can't be a revolutionary if you don't eat chillies...*" I'm not sure where that leaves us but it shows that it doesn't matter who you are or what you say, there is always someone who just has to make some smart-arse comment thinking it's funny! Could have been worse though; revolutionary Vietnam had Ho Chi Minh as their leader and he used to work on the Newhaven to Dieppe ferry as a pastry chef, so small mercies and all that! In short, if you like that sort of thing then read on, this story is right up your 'rue'.

Looking back, 2001 started off quite well. I was working for a company as a Regional Sales Manager based in London – Cannon Street to be precise – and had a team of 3 or 4 people working with me. I say 3 or 4 because the team was a bit of a moveable feast; some days 3 turned up for work (usual old cobblers...trouble on trains, car wouldn't start, had to take the kids to break into an old people's home...) sometimes there were 4.

What they didn't seem to comprehend is that I'd heard every excuse under the sun and knew it for what it was. They also forgot that I tended to use the very same trains and underground system that they did, and if I got there, well...FYI...Don't try and bullshit someone who does it for a living.

Trudy (wife of nine years as of 2001...still here today. Note to self: look on eBay for acceptable long service medal / Certificate for services to matrimony under extreme conditions or equivalent. If unavailable, buy doughnuts...always acceptable.) was working for a Japanese bank and, whilst our financial situation would hardly have made Jeff Bezos cast an envious eye in our direction, we were doing OK; not so much breadline as 'baked camembert and flat-bread' line. A couple of times a month we would rise up from our normal, mundane routine of Saturday morning at Sainsbury's, where people wandered around like retired Morlocks from H.G Wells 'Time Machine' living in some dystopian nightmare, and fought over the last floret of cauliflower whilst muttering "where's my loyalty card, where's my loyalty card" or "must...buy...chickens...two for one, two for one".

They man-handled their trolleys in the same way as they drove their cars; with reckless abandon and completely oblivious to other road/aisle users; displaying an ability, honed over years of practice, to abandon the aforementioned cars or trolleys in a way that made it strategically impossible to get past or avoid. It was like a retail version of the battle of Jutland!

They were ably assisted by tattooed and bearded individuals (…and that's just the women!), pushing buggies the size of small hatchbacks down the aisle with one hand, whilst attempting to stuff handfuls of Haribo's into the gaping mouths of screaming babies called Travis or Riocca. Any one of the above behaviours would have been enough to break a man but with them all working in partnership, it made our occasional trip to Waitrose seem like a weekend in the Cotswolds.

There were people there that looked like us, they looked normal; lovely fragrant people who smelt of aftershave and perfume instead of Brobat blue and toilet duck. They were sipping cappuccinos from refillable coffee cups and wearing proper shoes with soles and everything, instead of fluffy mule slippers or trainers. At one point I seriously considered asking the assistant on the deli counter (whose perfectly blemish free complexion looked like porcelain, and was in complete contrast to the woman on the fish counter at Sainsbury's who looked like she'd been set on fire and put out with a rake) if I could reserve a spot at the end of her counter for the last week of August/first week of September.

To make things even better (audience sighs collectively as they realise he's still going...), the lovely Trudy (see above) had booked us a really special trip away as a celebration of my 40th birthday. We were going on a four-day excursion to New York, staying at the Edison Hotel, an art deco hotel very close to Times Square...WHAT FUN!!... I'd been to the USA a couple of times before but Trudy hadn't and we couldn't wait.

We excitedly made a mental note of all the things we would like to do and then crossed those out and replaced them with all the things we wanted to eat. Our date of departure was racing towards us.

We both worked hard and the combination of 5.30am starts and 5.00pm finishes, contributed to us needing and looking forward to the break with much gusto. Lists were made, clothes were washed and ironed, I was allowed four old pairs of underpants to wear on rotation to keep all the 'good ones' *(Shock news!! blokes don't have GOOD and BAD pants... THEYRE ALL RANCID!!!)* for the trip. The big day arrived and the trip to New York was upon us. My 'Idiots guide to New York' guide book was diligently packed along with an emergency pack of Assam loose leaf tea - we're not savages after all – and off we went; the aim? To take a very large bite out of the Big Apple while I still had all my own teeth. I was looking forward to doing all the things tourists did; seeing the Empire state building, riding in the famous yellow cabs, consuming food to a level hitherto unknown to man and I'd heard that there was a deli near our hotel where the staff were particularly rude and sirly; I was looking forward to it immensely!! Indeed I complained to one of the staff at the aforementioned establishment when he asked me if everything was satisfactory that "..*I had heard that the staff could be surly and rude and that they had, in fact, been extremely polite and proficient in their duties..*" and that "*I'm not very happy about it!*" He looked at me slightly asconsed "*You Limeys! What is it with your sense of humour!!*"

The trip was everything we had hoped it would be; food by the bucket load, lots of "*…you have a nice day now…*" thrown around like confetti and we hit all the normal tourist hotspots – Central Park, Times Square, Madison Square Gardens and The Financial District to the south of the city. We didn't realise then how our lives were about to change.

When the first of the planes (United Airlines Flight 11) smashed into the North tower, no-one really understood what was happening. On the streets below, people were going about their everyday business and routines on what was a normal Tuesday morning. People were on their way to work, drinking coffee and chatting with friends. In offices, people were doing what they always did – chatting with colleagues, refilling photocopiers with paper; normal people just doing normal things. Everyone assumed it was a terrible accident.

When the second plane (United Airlines Flight 175) banked gently round from the distance and hit the South tower, live on TV, and the reports started flooding in of the third and fourth planes, one that had been deliberately crashed into the Pentagon and the other that had failed to reach its destination because of the unbelievably heroic actions of the passengers on board, everyone started to understand and realise that this was different and no accident. The world took a collective, sharp intake of breath as, in a matter of moments, it was changed beyond recognition and forever. Two days prior to the 9/11 attacks, Trudy and I had visited Lower Manhatten and the financial district where the World Trade Center buildings were situated. We had taken a trip on the Statten Island ferry, embarked on a sightseeing trip on the Hudson River and stood, posing for pictures up against the North tower. In search of relief from the summer sun, we had even taken in some retail shopping in the shopping mall built beneath two of the towers (4 and 5) of the World Trade Center complex, a shopping mall that was now crushed and destroyed by the collapsing towers; towers that were now a filthy, disfigured pile of molten metal and rubble, their parts twisted and mis-shapen from the impact and heat they had endured.

The Sunday prior to the attacks had been sweltering. Trudy and I had been walking around these very buildings and we had both wanted to visit the 'Windows of the World' restaurant at the very top of the North Tower. After a long day and, unable to find the main evelator to take us there, we decided against it. We made do with sitting in the piazza underneath the towers and relaxed in one of the cafes. There was a mezzanine that surrounded the piazza where you could walk and look down at the families relaxing and enjoying their weekend. For a Sunday it was quite busy with children running along the mezzanine and couples sharing a meal or a drink. We decided to go back to the hotel, freshen up and hit the bar in the hotel before going out to eat in Times Square. On the way to the Subway station to take us back to the hotel, we noticed a sign: 'WINDOWS OF THE WORLD RESTAURANT – 107th FLOOR' and an arrow directing us back to Tower 1 or North Tower. We decided that rather than retracing our steps, we would return and go to there for breakfast on the morning of our departure. Our return flight was booked for the morning of September 11th. The evening of 10th

September was a raucous affair; it was the last night of the holiday and we intended to go out with a bang. We had met and made friends with another couple in the hotel, Martin and Lyn, and the evening developed and descended into one of cocktails, drinks, laughter, cocktails, more laughter and…did I mention the cocktails?

For no other reason other than it's just not my thing, I don't drink. It's not because I try, in vain, to live a puritan life and those people that know me will attest to the fact that if my body was, indeed, a temple, then the pews have been empty for some time. I just don't do it. On the night of 10th September and, after a lot…and I do mean a lot… of booze, and, in a state of drunkenness for only the third time in my life, Martin, Lyn, Trudy and I poured ourselves into a taxi and headed 'uptown' for something to eat. In the early hours of 11th September we got back to the hotel and, after sneaking our way past the main desk as only four drunk people can do, "shooshing" each other and professing undying love for everyone we encountered, we got back to our room. Knowing that we were getting up early to go to the Windows of the World restaurant for breakfast prior to going to the airport and returning home, I set the alarm…or so I thought. After sleeping through the 7.30am alarm call, we woke and turned on the television. I was in the bathroom when Trudy told me that a plane had hit one of the twin towers. We stopped what we were doing and started watching the reporter relay the story and, as she did so, we could see the second plane, Flight 175, gently bank round in the distance, fly towards the camera and smash into the South Tower before disintegrating in a huge, searing fireball.

The world seemed to stop, we couldn't take in what was right in front of us…it couldn't be happening could it?

I'm not sure I believe in guardian angels – real ones not the beret adorned vigilante group that patrolled the London underground in the mid 1980's – but someone up there was looking out for us that night. All I know is that if we *hadn't* been worse for wear, If I *hadn't* been drunk for only the third time in my life, if I *hadn't* cocked up setting the 7.30 alarm and if we *hadn't*, as a consequence, overslept, we would have been eating breakfast at the top of the North Tower when the first plane struck. We would, most likely, have been dead; of that there is no doubt, and that is a very sobering thought and one that both sharpens your focus and gives you a whole new set of priorities.

We were locked down in New York for a further six days. All planes were grounded, all phone lines in and out of New York were overloaded. After managing to contact our families and let them know we were OK, we just sat tight and waited for news. The timing of the attacks meant that we were obliged to check out of our hotel on the morning of the attacks despite the whole world it seemed trying to re-book the rooms they had just vacated. At the time the only advice the British Consulate could give was to contact the YMCA to see if they had somewhere we could stay until we were able to get home. This advice seemed inadequate to say the least but in hindsight, what could they do? It was unprecedented. We decided to speak to the hotel to weigh up our options.

We had to check out as other guests had reserved our room but, as I explained to the Duty Manager, if we couldn't get out...they couldn't get in. The hotel and its staff were magnificent.

We were allowed to keep our room at 'rack rate' which is the lowest tariff they could do; "...*after all*" as the Duty Manager said "... *they had no intention of making a profit out of the situation...*"

The airlines had no idea when the airports would re-open and it became a daily ritual of phoning the airlines to ascertain the up to date situation.

The city itself felt numb during the six days that we were locked down; like a boxer that had taken a head shot and was vainly hanging on hoping to hear the bell at the end of the round. Physically, it looked like it had had its two front teeth knocked out and the days immediately following the attacks seemed to show the world a different side of New York. The real New York. A city of compassion and caring, of love and togetherness. Communities came together to grieve with, and for, each other, and there was a never ending stream of volunteers drawn together to help. In some cases it was by the smallest of actions, but people felt that they needed to do SOMETHING. In Times Square, every available inch of wooden building site facia board was taken up and dedicated to pictures of missing loved ones and family members with smiling, proud faces. Each one of them someone's mother, father, sister or brother; not CEO's of multi-national corporations, accountants or solicitors but innocent people; their lives cut short and their lights extinguished in a second of what was for them, just an ordinary working day. We were in limbo, Trudy and I just walked the streets trying to fill our days, not really knowing what to do or say. On the next street, the entire road and pavement were a carpet of yellow and red flowers; the colours a deliberate tribute to match the uniforms of the firefighters of the fire station on that street (**Engine 54/Ladder 4/Battalion 9)**, all of whom had responded to the emergency calls when they came in and all of whom had been killed when the towers collapsed. Restaurants closed their doors to the public and only opened to provide food, some fleeting respite and some solace to the emergency services.

If, by carrying out the attacks, the terrorists thought that the spirit of New York would be broken, then they failed… miserably. The attacks served only to strengthen the city's resolve and unite the people in one simple objective; to overcome and to rebuild - bigger, better and stronger, if for no other reason than to act as a tribute and a memorial to the people who died.

I'll always remember the moment when the airline finally said that the plane was going and that we had to be at the airport in 2 hours.

We rushed to claim our places on an airport transfer which the hotel had already arranged and once we arrived at the airport we were subjected to a seemingly infinite amount of new security checks before being allowed through to departures. I don't mind admitting that I was terrified but, as someone pointed out, if you were going to fly, now was the time to do it. Security had never been so tight, and the sight of seeing plane after plane take off and land without incident, to a backdrop of a long, curling plume of smoke that continually drifted across the Hudson river from the site of what was now being called Ground Zero, served to quell my fears. That, in tandem with the very large and very capable looking security staff that were being detailed to each flight; if they said they were out of peanuts, trust me, they were out of peanuts.

When we came back our lives had irreversably changed. Everyday issues seemed so irrelevant. How important was it that an order hadn't arrived on a specific day? Did it really matter that a meeting had been cancelled? In the grand scale of things no, not when the image scorched onto your brain was that of people throwing themselves from the hundreth floor of a building to avoid being burnt to death....not one bit.

On our return, we were initially met with a slight problem. Our car was parked at Gatwick Airport...in Surrey, problem was that we had landed at Stansted Airport...in Essex.

This issue however had been abley dealt with by my 75 year old mother who, on hearing of our predicament, had telephoned the company that looked after the parking at Gatwick and had, in her best telephone voice (oh come on! We've all got one!) relayed our plight to the poor, unsuspecting member of staff on the other end of the telephone line. It was such a shame...his day had started off so well!

Mum had explained what had happened and the conversation continued, liberally interspersed with "I'm sure you are aware of the situation"...."unavoidable delay"...you get the picture. It was at this point that 'Phil' (that's not his name but for the sake of the story just go with it) from

Pink Elephant parking, saw his day go RAPIDLY downhill. He explained to mother that "…whilst he understood the circumstances, there was nothing he could do" and that "there would be a surcharge based on the six extra days parking that had been taken" …BIG mistake. At that point mother apologised for her bad language and launched into a tirade that turned foul language into an art form. Poor Phil..he was clearly not used to dealing with, and was in NO WAY prepared or trained to enter verbal gymnastics with a 75-year old Jewish mother whose only son had nearly died in what was now know to be the worst terrorist attack in memory. He was reminded that if he continued with this line of response she would have no option but to not only contact the head office and demand to know why they had A) not allowed their staff to make fundamental business decisions so that it didn't seem as though they had aligned themselves to extremist terrorism B) insisted on making a profit from the situation, but also C) when someone would be available to answer these and other questions from the local newspapers.

For those of you who may have watched 'The Good Life' and remember the scene where Margot Leadbetter discusses her council tax in the Tax Office with the chap behind the screen? I'll leave it with you. Mother had gone full 'Margot' and, under those circimstances there was only one option. Run for your lives.

When I arrived at Gatwick airport short-term parking the following day, I was met by a very nice operative who said that "…Phil would have loved to have met me in person this morning" but that "…he was off sick today with a stress related illness" I apologised on behalf of my family and collected my car…free of charge of course…before exiting 'stage left' very quickly but being very careful to adhere to all speed restrictions as I did so.

Arriving back in the relative calm of the UK seemed almost surreal and the events of the previous week seemed as though they were part of some unbelievable nightmare. The more you thought about it, the more it seemed unconscionable that people would plot to carry out such an atrocious act of terrorism. But they had and now we all had to live with the consequences. Trudy had a call from her boss who ordered her to take a few days off to get things back to some semblance of normality which, wisely, she took. I, on the other hand, decided I was OK and the next day went into work in my office in Cannon Street. I wasn't OK; not in the slightest.

For the majority of the time, I worked alone and had too much time to contemplate what had happened and what we had been through. Stress is a strange thing that creeps up on you when you don't expect it and you reach a tipping point that sends you over the edge. It could be a completely innocuous thing…spilling a drink on your trousers or similar but it would be enough to send you into a deluge of tears and a smothering feeling of panic and depression would descend over you like a thick fog, enveloping you to the point where you couldn't see a way out or how you were going to get through it.

Gradually, over a period of about six months, things got better and reverted back to routine. It became easier to put the events of New York further back in our memories; not forgotten but more able to be dealt with. By now it was coming up to early summer of 2002, and we had planned a trip with our friends Ian and Jen and their new baby son Tom to the Dordogne region of France, staying in a self-catering cottage near Aubeterre.

We chose France as it was relatively near and, most importantly, driveable, as Ian was afraid of flying. We arrived and soon made ourselves at home, settling in to a strict regime of eating, laughing and drinking. So committed were we to the regime, that on more than one occasion the proprietor, a portly English chap who lived next door, would look over the fence or pop round to make sure no one had been murdered such was the howls and screams emanating from our cottage. In our opinion it was either that or he just wanted to cop a look at the girls in their swimming gear…at least I hope it was the girls. It was a great holiday and the break was just what we needed. During the holiday and over the odd glass of red, the four of us mooted the idea of buying a couple of places somewhere in France, close enough that we could drive to for a long weekend, with a view that perhaps long-term we would move over full time and try to get back to doing what WE wanted to do instead of continually treading the path that the working treadmill had dictated. Ian was self-employed as a plasterer, and a very good one as well and, whilst Trudy and I both had secure jobs, we were not afraid of a challenge so the plan was hatched. We decided that once we got back home, we would start to look for somewhere suitable - finances permitting - and if it needed renovation then with Ian's building skills and my elementary 'but with a strong desire to learn' DIY skills, then so be it. We knew the area we wanted, we had a budget, it was *'Tous les systèmes sont prêts!'*

To be honest, up to that point, my experience of France was based around a couple of holidays in the 80s and my overall opinion of France and the French in general was the same as millions of other people; take 'em or leave 'em and I could do without their slightly superior Gallic attitude where they looked at me with a mixture of contempt and condolence because I wasn't French. To be fair, they had every right to give me the 'long lunette'. After all, France was (and still is) the most popular holiday destination in the world. It had everything. From the glitz and glamour of Paris with its shops, bars, café and restaurant culture (not to mention the Parisians themselves who seemingly have to serve a 2-year apprenticeship in 'arseiness' and who still regard splitting your French infinitives or improper use of the past participle as punishable by the guillotine) and the sun-kissed beaches of Cannes in the south, to the snow-covered peaks of the French Alps and the small traditional fishing towns of the Atlantic coast, their fully laden boats burgeoning with shrimps, prawns, lobsters and other such nautical niceties.

As our budget dictated, Trudy and I had been looking in the agreed area, which we had decided amongst us was going to be the Atlantic Coast and, in particular, La Rochelle or the surrounding area. What we wanted was a small traditional house (X2) to use as a holiday getaway; far enough for it to feel like a break but not too far to take too long to get to. Prices were cheap (still are compared to UK house prices!) and this price difference was ameliorated by the fact that you got €1.42 to the pound!!...I know, halcyon days indeed! Trudy had always nurtured a passion for cooking, hence my expanding waistline, and had long harboured a dream to run a provincial 'chambres d'hote' in rural France.

Her job was part-time and gave her more holiday flexibility to search for potential houses so, in order to find a suitable place, she would arrange to see maybe 3 or 4 houses in the same area, arrange a trip and nip over to see them, spending a couple of days in the process 'reccying' the area, then nip back again and report back as to which ones were worth consideration. This particular method of house searching seemed to work well for us and, as we weren't in a major rush, over the next year or so we took our time, confident that something would, eventually, turn up.

I would like to think that I had some form of influence over this decision-making process but I'm a realist if nothing else and knew that I was being consulted purely for aesthetic purposes only and that it was an administrative exercise and nothing else. I used to nod in the right places, stroke my chin and emit a noise like "mmm" to make it seem like I was interested, and show interest using my best furrowed brow look; If I was feeling REALLY brave I would throw in comments like "that barn roof looks like it might need a bit of attention" or "could be nice if we moved the bath/toilet/bed/wardrobe (insert as appropriate) to here" but in my heart of hearts I reconciled myself to the fact that I was but a passenger in the grand scale of things. Normally the debrief was a very truncated affair and consisted of me saying "any good?" and the answer being "no, not really" for some reason or other. Now all of this was taking place at a time when Ryanair had temporarily stopped flying into Limoges (early to mid 2003) and as part of her latest trip, Trudy was forced to fly into Lyon, south east of La Rochelle by about 5 hours, and drive across to the Charente-maritime region where La Rochelle could be found. The following day, whilst wiling away the hours in my office and wondering what form my evening meal would take, or more accurately, whose house could I go to for dinner while Trudy was away, my phone rang; it was Trudy…

-*"Hello love, all OK?"*

- *"Yep not bad. Just wanted to update you on the houses I've seen today"*

-*"OK" I said nervously. Why was she PHONING me with an update? I was sweating up a bit…this wasn't the normal procedure. This was highly irregular..*

-*"Well I didn't actually get to La Rochelle"*

-*"Right"* I said. An air of trepidation was starting to engulf me and there was definitely a whiff of uncertainty in the air. I knew I shouldn't have had the egg sandwich.

-*"Where DID you get to?"* I enquired, nervously.

"I'm in a department called Creuse, it's in the Limousin region"

I was none the wiser, my geographical knowledge of France was non-existant.

"where's that?" I asked *"give me a clue"*

"It's further south than we were looking, about two hours north-west of Lyon, and I was on my way to La Rochelle, but had to come through this region and I don't want to go any further. This is it Mark, this is where I want to be!"

"Right!" I said, somewhat taken aback by Trudy's positive demeanour and her willingness to change the agreed plan without so much as an Extraordinary General Meeting being arranged or a corum being formed for decision making purposes.

-*"Anyway I saw a few places today and none of them were any good"*.

-*"O..kay....so why are you phoning me then?"*

-*"Well I say none of them, there was one that I think might be quite good"*.

Trudy told me about the house; what it had, what it needed. Importantly the price was good and I had to admit it did sound interesting.

-*"Well if you think it's the one and there are other people interested then perhaps we should speak to the bank and think about speaking to the agent about it"*

-*"I already have"* says she…*"I've bought it"*

If you could collectively cast your eyes back up the page, the more attentive of you will see that my contribution to the house buying process was, by mutual agreement and understanding, largely ceremonial and I'm not really sure why I was surprised at this turn of events as this wasn't exactly Trudy's debut at this sort of thing. The house in Braintree we were living in at the time? bought whilst I was on a training course. Indeed our current house-purchased 'sans-moi' while I was working in the UK.

In general when women say "I'm going shopping" it barely registers on the male radar and certainly not if there is any form of televised sport afoot. When Trudy says "I'm off shopping" My sphincter sucks onto the chair like a limpet mine and I start hyperventilating at the potential implications. I'm as likely to get a 'pied-a-terre' as I am pomme de terre.

For the uninitiated, the house buying process in France is significantly easier and less stressful than in the UK. Firstly, it is the purchaser that pays the agents fees and, normally, these fees are included within the price of the house. Secondly, if you agree to pay the full asking price, the seller is legally obliged to accept AND remove the house from the market. Thirdly – and perhaps most significantly – once you have signed the pre-contract agreement to buy the house (compromis de vente) you then have a period of time (7,10 or 14 days as agreed) to change your mind. Once this has elapsed and you have transferred the deposit monies over to the solicitor, the house is, because of the slightly more 'user friendly' process, ostensibly yours. You do, of course have to navigate the legal process but this is normally a singularly uneventful process and a couple of months later you become a european home owner. No surveys, no gazumping, no changing of minds on a whim – all rather boring if truth be told. I mean, who doesn't enjoy the frisson of excitement that courses through your body as you try to determine if the fluff on the ceiling means the roof's going to collapse or the two line report from a surveyor, down valuing your intended purchase, who lives 200 miles away from the house you intend to buy, but insists he knows the market as well as the agent who's worked the area for 20 years and has priced - AND SOLD - hundreds of similar properties. After all it's only probably the single biggest investment you will ever make, and his valuation is based on whether or not he remembered to put his two-stage ladder in the car to allow him to get access to the loft hatch! Anyway…I digress… a few months after seeing the house, it was ours.

I can't remember a specific conversation where Trudy and I discussed the issue, but shortly after returning from our holiday in France with Ian and Jen in 2002, we had decided it was time to follow our hearts and make a leap of faith. As we had learnt in New York, you never knew what life had in store for you just around the next corner. What had started as a plan to have a holiday home took on a whole new perspective and a life of its own. We were going to start again and do what WE wanted. We would move to France – lock, stock and barrel, start up a bed and breakfast as we had aways dreamed and live our lives on our terms. After discussing the change in plan with Ian and Jen and over the course of the intervening months, Ian and Jen had reconsidered their options and had decided that they didn't feel they were ready to up sticks and leave the UK on a permanent basis. They had welcomed another baby to the family (...everyone, please welcome Tom's little brother James to the world!...) and they felt that they wanted to be based in the UK where their support network was more easily accesible. We completely understood, but ploughed on none the less. The bombshell they dropped on us though, was that they wanted to buy our house. With that in mind, by the time we signed for our house in France in July 2003, we had already sold our house in the UK.

Bizarrely, the area in which we had found - and purchased - the house, wasn't completely unknown to Trudy. On investigation it transpired that she had, as a child, visited the area with her sister, Tracey, to stay with family friends, Lanny and Claude who lived in a small village called La Pouge. It was in fact during one of these summer sojourns that Trudy had been introduced to and started a long standing affair with alcohol – Sambucca to be more precise. It is a love affair that has stood the test of time and shows absolutley no sign of abaiting! Some days I think its particularly reckless for her to stand near an open fire but, having seen what she becomes once she's had a few 'liveners', I'm certainly not going to be the one to tell her! Having kicked abstinence firmly out of the door, sent it running down the path with a firm "...*and don't come back!*..." ringing in its ears, and taken the first steps towards insobriety, Trudy and Tracey reciprocated by introducing Lanny and Claude's son to baked beans on toast. Unfortunately baked beans as we know them are the somewhat weaker version of the french equivalent. In the absence of the popular british variety, Claude offered to make a french version using flagelet beans in a tomato sauce. The resulting tsunami of flatulance served not only to break down any protocol or etiquette barriers that still existed, but also served to send their son on an enforced, extended period in bed, sprinkled with frequent visits to the lavatory to try and expel some of the noxious, fetid gases that were being produced. At one point, things got so bad that the military took readings that confirmed their suspicions that the atmosphere around the kitchen could have been legally weaponised and used to repel an invading army had it not been for the Geneva Convention.

La Pouge itself was only about 20 minutes from the house we had bought, our house being in a hamlet called Grand Villard which was part of the larger commune of St Hilare La Plaine. This meant that with a bit of brushing up on geography, Trudy pretty soon started to remember the local area. A good effort I thought bearing in mind it was probably the first time she'd seen the area sober.

The house in Grand Villard was owned by a couple who were, unfortunately, divorcing. The husband had moved out leaving his wife, Rose, and their two children, Nicolas and Melanie in the house while their divorce went through and became final. After the house had become legally ours in July 2003, we made a couple of trips over to ensure all was OK but, as we had now come to winter, we saw no benefit in doing anything until Spring 2004 and, as the decision had been made to make the move to France permanent, and as we had already, in essence, sold our house to Ian and Jen, our plan was to make the big move in May 2004. In our best broken french, we asked Rose what her plans were and it became apparent that it suited both parties if she stayed in the house until we were ready to move over. She was delighted with this agreement and we came back to the UK comforted by the fact the house would be occupied over the winter months; months that in Creuse could be harsh and quite severe.

Snow was a very regular occurrence and temperatures could send the mercury plummeting down to -10 or sometimes colder. As my dad would say…"perishing".

The sale of our house in Braintree, Essex, was going well. Ian and Jen were keen to complete as soon as they could and we all estimated that we would be ready to exchange contracts and complete the sale of the house in early 2004. This meant that we would need to vacate our house before moving over to France, and would spend a couple of months at my parents house as a stop gap.

Two months…maximum - definitely no longer. Just two…..long….months.

I don't fully understand what happened but in September 2003 the sale of our house in Braintree completed and we found ourselves moving out; some four months EARLER than planned! This meant that we had the opportunity to reflect for a moment, collectively stroke our chins in a thoughtful manner whilst muttering "..hmmm…", draw slowly on the end of an imaginary pipe and consider that we now had the chance to spend not TWO but SIX – that's… SIX! - MONTHS at my parents house, a 3 bedroom (although one was used as a sitting room) bungalow in Rayleigh, near to Southend-on-Sea. I knew Southend-on-Sea from when I was a child; we would pack some sandwiches and some drinks into a picnic and set off excitedly on family excursions to the seaside.

We always knew we were getting close when we went past what we used to call the 'spring onion' which was in fact the chimney of a factory on an industrial estate on the A127. I still have no idea what the factory was but I do know that is wasn't a real spring onion. The journey to Southend on Sea was always broken up by my dad declaring that it was 'time for a brew up' once we reached Redbridge Station and we would invariably stop in a layby somewhere on the eastbound carriageway near the Halfway House pub whereupon the camping gas stove would come out along with a small kettle and provisions for making tea. Once father was replete we would continue onward. For those who are not aware of, or who have never been to Southend on Sea, it can be found a few miles east of Basildon on the Thames estuary and is famed for having the longest pier in the world at just over a mile long. Noted Southend-on-Sea 'alumni' include star of screen and stage, Dame Helen Mirren, COUNTDOWN mathematician Rachel Riley and former UK number 1 tennis player John Lloyd. Famous (but useless) Southend-on-Sea facts include the fact that parts of the town were featured in the 1964 James Bond film Goldfinger. James Bond who was played by Sean Connery at the time drives into

Southend Airport in his Aston Martin DB5 following Auric Goldfinger onto a plane!

Whilst I had enjoyed the facilities that Southend-on-Sea had to offer as a child; I mean who wouldn't revel in the delights of Peter Pan's playground on the main seafront or the putting green at Westcliff-on-Sea, not to mention the cockle and whelk stalls oft' frequented by my father at Leigh-on-Sea, as an adolescent, going out for a night out to T.O.T.S (Talk Of The South) on Southend seafront filled a young, inexperienced bloke with a nervous kind of dread; the women were fierce and the only thing that set them apart from their male counterparts was that most of the women had a higher sperm count. Rumour (and it was only rumour alas!) had it that you could always tell when a Southend girl was sexually excited because they dropped their chips! there was a reason its acronym was SOS!

And so, dear reader, we find ourselves ensconced at mum and dad's place and, during the time we spent 'chez parents' and as our moving day duly arrived, it began to dawn on us the monumental change that we were about to make in our lives. We decided that discretion was the better part of valour and, whilst I trusted my boss to be understanding to our situation and our overall plan, it could be regarded as dereliction of duty if he knew I was leaving and knowingly made no plan for my succession.

It was unfair to say anything and we decided that 'plausible deniability' suited all concerned; in other words, keep your mouth shut and tell NO-ONE!

I planned to resign and give the customary four weeks notice of leaving my job, at the end of February 2004. This would give us a full 6-8 weeks to get our affairs finally in order before departing these shores in May 2004. It would also give my company enough time to arrange a successor and any handover time required. We didn't even tell our respective companies that we had moved house.

Around January of 2004 it became harder and harder to concentrate on my work and my role, without seeing the figurative 'chequered flag' in the distance. It became noticeable and my Sales Director, Adam, whose brother Ben was the MD, asked to see me to chat over what had changed. When I met with him, I decided to tell him, albeit unofficially, what was going on. Once he had wiped the remnants of his tuna and sweetcorn sandwich off of the counter at the sandwich bar and stopped coughing, I told him why we were going and told him that I planned to resign – officially - at the end of February and that if he tried to force me to leave prior to that date I would deny the conversation had ever taken place. He agreed and I went back to my office, strangely relieved that I had been able to share the load with someone.

About a week later, the phone rang. It was my MD. I liked Ben, even if he hadn't been my boss I think I would want him as a mate.

"Wainy! What are you doing at the end of Feb" he asked

My heart developed a panic induced arrhythmia and I told myself to keep calm. Surely Adam hadn't said anything. He wouldn't…would he?

"nothing as far as I'm aware Ben…why?" I replied, the pitch of my voice unnaturally high due to nerves.

"I wondered if you would be open to going to an industry conference as our company representative? It's a residential conference over a 10 day period. Obviously we would pay your expenses and I just need you to go to a couple of seminars. The rest of the time is yours and of course you can take Trudy with you"

I knew there was a conference every year on the south coast where middle-aged industry representatives wearing 50% polyester suits and non-iron shirts drank too much and discussed the many new and exciting innovations being promoted by the paper and pencil manufacturers from around the globe…as you can imagine I couldn't wait….what an opportunity. Let me put that another way, I literally could not think of anything I wanted to do less than this…literally nothing.

"..Where is it Ben ?" I said with some trepidation, trying to think how I was going to break the news to Trudy that we were going to be spending 10 days in Bournemouth...or, put another way that *I,* and *I alone,* would be spending 10 days in Bournemouth as the chances of me getting Trudy to come with me were about as high as the next Pope being Jewish.

"Barbados" came the reply.

"Sorry Ben, for a minute there I thought you said Barbados"

"Yes, I did...Barbados " he repeated.

Well slap me thrice and call me mother!... This was a turn-up for the trousers. I found myself in a dicotemy, could we actually go on the trip, come back as though all was well and then I resign? No...it wouldn't be right. I'm a firm believer that you should be careful who you tread on when going up the career ladder as you never know if you might need to step on them again when you're on the way down. And with the outcome or success of our plan to start a new life in France far from assured, coming back having given it a bash but failing magnificently was a distinct possibility.

"..can I have a chat with Trudy and get back to you tomorrow?" I asked, *"...got a few things going on at*

present and just need to run it up the flag pole but in any case, thanks for the opportunity"

"no worries Wainy...speak tomorrow"

I put the phone down and put my head in my hands
"...Oh BOLLOCKS!!!!!! " I shouted through my
entwined fingers; how was I going to explain this to
the memsahib and, more importantly, how was I
going to tell her we couldn't go!!

The ensuing conversation with Trudy explaining the
situation went better than I could have hoped for.
Luckily the attention I had paid during Mrs Johnson's
Home Economics classes and, in particular, the
needlework part of the curriculum, meant that sowing
my knackers back on using a blunt darning needle
was a much less painful experience than I had
imagined.

I did have to explain to Trudy a couple of times why
we couldn't go but, finally, we agreed that it would be
wrong to go knowing that we had plans of our own
for the end of February, and we hatched a plan that
would get us off the hook.

The following day I arrived at my office in Cannon
Street early. I knew Ben always got into his office early
and I wanted to have the conversation with him
straight away and not sit there contemplating it before
eventually losing my nerve and not phoning.

When I spoke to him he was, as always, on good form;

"...Wainy! How are you ol' boy? Still a tosser?"

"Yep! Pretty much boss! Anyway, just wanted to talk to you about this conference"

"Yeah good...got to be honest I was a bit surprised that you needed some time to think about it!"

"I know but you caught me on the hop a bit and I needed to give it some thought overnight because there's an issue.."

"an issue?... what issue?"

"Ben I'm really sorry but since the whole New York thing I just can't fly...I'm terrified to be honest...absolutely shit myself when I think of going on a plane and Barbados? Well that's a long flight! That's why Trudy and I have been going to France for holidays since it happened...we can drive there you see!"

"Oh shit- Wainy! I didn't even give it a thought! No worries, fair play, no worries at all"

"I just wanted to let you know as soon as possible so that you could give the chance to someone else"

"Yeah – great – brilliant – thanks for letting me know..."

Somewhere in a reception area at a Japanese bank near St.Paul's station, a receptionist named Trudy was weeping silently into her 'mocca frappaccino with an extra shot' as she realised that her 10 day all expenses paid trip to Barbados was no more…all because I had morals!

The bruises healed much quicker than I anticipated they would after being beaten about the body by a four-slice electric toaster, but eventually Trudy calmed down. As you would imagine, I did have to pick my moments to speak to her for a few days (of course by days dear reader, I mean weeks) and would invariably signal that I wanted to enter into a conversation by offering her my hand to sniff whilst uttering *"…easy girl!…easy!…friend!…I only want to talk…"*

Eventually we reached the end of February and I resigned, informing Ben, that the whole 'scared of flying' thing was, in fact, a ruse but necessary to avoid putting him in an unenviable position. He agreed *"…you're a very nice man…"* he said, which was his way of saying that he was grateful for my subterfuge and so, as planned, I left the corporate world at the start of March 2004 with decisions to make and plans afoot. A couple of months later, with the contents of our house in a storage unit and with the removal company ready to go, the big day arrived.

We were moving to France…what could possibly go wrong.

Chapter 2 - Arrival

The day of our departure consisted of Trudy and I getting up bright and early and making our way over to the storage unit where the contents of our house had been stored for the last 7 months. We were met there by Trudy's parents, Evelyn and Reg, her sister Tracey and Tracey's partner Gary, known affectionately as Baxter...for no other reason other than that was his name; not particularly inventive but what do you care. We had had a 'last night' dinner with my family the night before and, not being one for long, sentimental goodbyes and hanky waving - after all we were British and an outpouring of emotions was simply not done - we jumped in the car and we were off. Lips of the upper variety remained stiff and any moisture found within the ocular region was generally noted as being an allergy of some description. With that in mind, when we were ready to go, mum and dad came to see us off at the front door with a muted "...*give us a ring when you get there...*" you could have been forgiven in thinking that when we left, we were going to Sainsbury's as opposed to starting a new life in France...only 22 miles away in geographical terms but a million miles away in terms of culture, language and a thousand other things.

Trudy and I had invested some time in French language evening classes at the local college but these didn't really work out as most of the people there had enrolled to give them some respite from their other half or children or both...one chap freely admitted that when he enrolled, he thought it was for French polishing!

Despite the fact that none of the other class members had turned up carrying a sideboard or bow-legged table, he continued to come, mainly for the tea and biscuits at half-time. This arrangement didn't really work for Trudy and I; primarily because you only ever progress at the speed of the slowest person and secondly because the teacher was a self-obsessed twat who would turn up when she wanted and then demand we all stay late to finish off the evening's work. As I pointed out to her in the most diplomatic manner I could muster after having completed a full day's work in Cannon St, that if we could get from Central London having been forced to sit or stand with the 'great unwashed' on the tube system, whilst being perilously close to asphyxia due to the proximity of a warm, moist, third party owned armpit, followed by the undertaking of a 45 minute drive from Redbridge station to Chelmsford, and STILL arrive at the allotted time, the very least she could do in return was cook her children's fish-fingers half an hour earlier and leave herself enough time to get from Springfield to Chelmsford town centre; a journey of about 10 minutes!

Apparently, I was being unreasonable so we left and started private lessons with a lady who wore huge slippers that looked like stuffed cats and who refused to speak English to us from the moment we walked in her front door to the time we left. Both of these things - especially the slippers - I found much more to my liking and we therefore continued to see her on a weekly basis for about 4 months prior to our departure. By the time we left for France, our French was by no means conversant and certainly not error free, but frankly, if I went into a 'boulangerie' for bread and came out with bread, I was happy.

Anyway, I digress. Having left the storage unit at about 10.30am, we agreed with the driver of our transport lorry, Alec, that the first stop of the day would be once we got to Calais and we could then agree on the route we intended to take. In actual fact, the first stop of the day was just shy of Thurrock services when his lorry got a puncture.

Rather than see this as a sign of things to come, we hurriedly helped him change the offending tyre and resumed our journey. Our plan was to get across the English Channel and then hot-foot it down to the house, about 7 hours with the route we were taking, and prepare for Alec's arrival a few days later. Tracey and Baxter were going to follow on the following day in their own car, stay for a few days to help us unpack and settle in before returning home, by which time Alec and his lorry would be well on their way back on the return trip. We got to Dover and before we knew it, we could see the white cliffs disappearing behind us into the distance along with our old lives.

I gave them a cheery 'adieu' from the stern of the ferry, strangely at ease and not filled with any anxiety or concern about what we were undertaking.

When we docked at Calais, we excitedly marked on the map the route we were going to take, double-checked that the heavily laden trailer – the metal framework for which had been recently refurbished and painted pea - green by Trudy's enthusiastic father - was safely attached and off we went.

Not really enthralled at the prospect of tackling the 'Periferique' motorway that surrounded Paris – the French version of the M25 but where everyone drove round it 'the wrong way' - we had decided on a more scenic route to the west of France.

The route took us from Calais and Boulogne, down to Rouen – worry not dear reader, the irony of us being on the 'road to Rouen' was not lost on us – where Joan of Arc was awoken one day by some very large men in robes and hoods who asked her *"Err…don't suppose you could do the honours and cut the ribbon on the town's*

new wood burning central heating system could you..."
upon which she picked up her box of Ye Olde Swan
Vestas, before being told *"not sure you'll need thermal
socks where you're going love"*

From Rouen the route took us down and through a
small provincial town called, Evereux, continuing
towards Dreux, Chatres, Orleans and Vierzon where
we picked up the A20 South to the Limousin region.
We finally parted company with the A20 at junction
23 which led us east towards the 'capital' and biggest
town in la Creuse – Gueret. 15 minutes further south
of Gueret and our journey came to an end. We were
now in the heart of the Limousin region...our new
home.

All was well, the trailer and its contents, noticeably a
very large and heavy De Dietrich cooker, had made it
in one piece and we decided on a few hours rest prior
to unpacking. Surprisingly, and with many hands
making the proverbial 'light work' of the task, it
wasn't long before everything was unloaded.

Alec the van driver arrived a day or so later and before
long we had unloaded the rest of our chattels and they
had been diligently delivered to the appropriate
room/rooms in the house. Alec did a very quick
turnaround and started the trip back, Tracey and
Baxter spent a couple of days with us looking over our
new house, barns and garden before they too headed

back north and back to Blighty. Finally, we were on our own and the enormity of it all started to hit home. Our minds were taken off of things by a mixture of adrenalin, blind ignorance and enthusiasm, and the sheer amount of work required to get the house how we wanted it and finished in time for the impending holiday season and the opening of our 'chambres de hotes'.

Chapter 3 - Wish we were here...Oh! we are!

Grand Villard was a lovely village; full of friendly neighbours who waved to us cheerily when we saw them and greeted us with a happy "bonjour" whenever they walked past. In the early days we were somewhat of a novelty. We were the first English people to live in the ST HILAIRE LA PLAINE commune and neighbours would look at us with a mixture of bewilderment and wonder as we ploughed into the renovation work and I fell off of ladders...and a number of other things if truth be told. To them, having English residents in the commune was a bit of a novelty. It was something they had never seen before...a little bit like when China sent their two pandas, Tian Tian and Yiang Guan to Scotland to live in Edinburgh Zoo and the local residents came in their droves to witness two of nature's finest creatures willingly eating fresh vegetables.

Our elected 'Maire' was Guy Jallot, who lived directly opposite us in Grand Villard with his wife Marthe. Both Guy and Marthe were lovely and an absolute godsend, helping us to integrate into the local community and introducing us to local artisans, many of who also remain close friends to this day. Our neighbours included Patrick Percevault, a plumber who spoke indecipherable French at us from day one, and who I am no nearer to fully understanding today, 17 years later, than I was on the day we arrived in France.

He spoke to us like he was firing french words at us out of a cannon…in true Morecombe and Wise /Andre Previn style, '…all the right words but not necessarily in the right order…'

We also had Didi, a 92-year-old chap; typical Creuseois who Patrick had 'adopted' as a surrogate father and made sure he wanted for nothing. Didi had inherited his house from his parents and had lived in the same house, which became the marital home and with whom he spent a number of happy years with his now sadly departed wife, since he was 2 years old! We also had a dentist and his wife and a doctor and his wife, Monsieur and Madame Giraubit, affectionately known as Cosmo and Mrs Lettuce; mainly because he looked like one of the characters from the popular '80s film MOONLIGHT starring Cher and Nicolas Cage, and barely a day passed without Mrs 'Cosmo' knocking on our front door and offering us a fresh, home-grown lettuce from their veggie patch. Mrs Giraubit wasn't alone in her attempts to pass off surplus items of salad and vegetables; on more than one occasion we would open our front door to be confronted by a huge, burgeoning basket of beautiful fresh, home-grown produce. Nothing was expected in return; just friendship. It was just their way of welcoming us to their village and this simple gesture was hugely appreciated and made our introduction to French life much easier and the transition much smoother.

Other residents included an accountant and his family (the daughter of whom was a bona fida genius and took her baccalaureate when she was about 10 years old (…she probably went on to do open heart surgery in her lunch break and now lives with a house full of cats…) and an eccentric, and in no small part terrifying, woman called 'Madame Tap-Tap' who lived in a small house at the end of the village, wore a goatskin coat regardless of the weather, that looked like it had been cut from its previous owner using a spoon, and could be heard walking down the road accompanied by a couple of mangey looking dogs, tapping her walking stick as she went…tap….tap…tap. The sound of walking stick on tarmac was like a starter's pistol to the residents and the precursor to anyone who was on the road at that time making a dash for the sanctuary of their own homes. She was, of course, quite mad; of this there was no question.

Her slightly skewed mental equilibrium was as a result of an argument with her husband 30 years previously, which ended with him taking one of the hunting rifles he kept in the house, walking out into the middle of the road outside their house,

shouting "...I'LL SHOW YOU!"...and blowing his brains out....some people just MUST have the last word...

As one resident once said "she's traumatised three generations of children in this village and shows no sign of stopping soon"

Life at Grand Villard soon settled down from the furore of our arrival as 'les anglais' became less of a tourist attraction. Just before we left the UK we had started a small business, Limousin Property Care, looking after people's holiday homes. Generally, this entailed gardening, small building works and larger project management. We had been fortunate enough to pick up a couple of clients just prior to leaving, and this started to take up more of our time as the business started to grow. During this period (2004 onwards) there was an increasing number of Brits who, on seeing how reasonably priced French property was in comparison to UK house prices and with the exchange rate steady at €1.42 to £1.00, had decided to invest in the French property market and become European house and landowners. The Limousin region was no different and it saw a rise in overall house purchases, and by foreign owners in particular, who tended to be more open to spending money on renovation work and upgrading their homes. This situation wasn't universally welcomed as it made it impossible for the local population to afford the rising prices based on their lower salaries and made the properties unaffordable. It was good however, for Limousin Property Care, as more and more people who, having entered into a legally binding contract or having bought their dream property, suddenly realised they needed someone to look after it for the 48 weeks a year that they weren't there!

A house in the middle of nowhere, sitting in 5 acres of countryside is very common in Creuse and seems very attractive if you live most of the year in a 3-bed terraced house in Bolton. However there seemed to be a job lot of epiphanies when people reached Calais when they realised they had neither the time nor the means to look after it. Shockingly, the grass doesn't stop growing just because you are not there. Amazingly we found people who under normal circumstances would shudder at the thought of painting a bedroom without taking advice, suddenly believed they had morphed into Tommy Walsh (…waits as reader tilts head, thinks wistfully and reminisces about popular '90s TV programme GROUND FORCE) when faced with the complete renovation of a 5-bedroomed stone farmhouse with attached barn!

Occasionally we would be asked to help someone in the village with some indeterminate task; cutting a hedge, chopping wood etc, mainly because we had the required equipment, but also if it needed tackling with a bit of good ol' British 'oomph'. One such occasion involved Patrick asking me if I could meet him at one of his worksites to help him remove a bath from the upper floors of a client's house. Patrick had his own business and employed another senior plumber, Alain, whose working day started at 8.00am and who could be seen thrashing his Citroen Xantia through the village at 7.59 at about 90kph to get to Patrick's house on time.

Alain was never knowingly without a roll-up on his lip and for a man of his age...60-ish...had the most luxurious head of lustrous black hair I had ever seen. Whilst this may have been due, in part, to a healthy French diet of 40 Citanes an hour and black coffee, I fear it had more to do with the extensive and liberal use of Grecian 2000 on a daily basis. Alain was accompanied to jobs by Patrick's son Kevin, I know - strange name for a Frenchman but who are we to judge... who was about 17 and was so thin you could see through his chest. He weighed less than my sandwiches. Between them they had about 1-1.5 PSI of 'heft' so I was asked if I could accompany them to assist in the removal of the bath. When I arrived on site, there was much chin scratching and arm waving taking place. Alain, in a surprise to everyone…sorry let me rephrase that, Alain, in a surprise to absolutely no-one, was re-lighting his rollup that he had already relit 3 times and Patrick was calculating how to get the bath down the two flights of stairs that had a 180 degree turn halfway down.

We were accompanied on this particular job by one of Patrick's friends who insisted on calling me "comrade" as he did everyone he met whose name he didn't know…bit like "mate" or "buddy" in UK.

There appeared to be a tried and trusted method for calculating a) whether or not we would accomplish the task at hand and b) the timescales to complete the task.

Mass x dimensions x number of Frenchman / 33% (as at least a third of them would just watch) was my theory. This turned out to be reasonably sound as "Comrade" decided his role was to direct us down the stairs from below. The bath itself was of cast iron variety and the plan was that while I lifted one end at the top, Alain and the pipe-cleaner that was Kevin would lift the bottom end of the bath as it went down the stairs. After agreeing the process would be "…une…deux…trois…LEVEZ" we collectively assembled into our allotted positions. Between verbally agreeing the lifting procedure and taking up their position at one end of the bath, Alain and the pipe cleaner managed to confuse each other as to whether there was a gap between the TROIS and LEVEZ or whether we were actually lifting on TROIS! They each had their own theory which meant that as I lifted one end, Alain synchronised his lift with me but the pipe cleaner didn't with the result being that the bath careered down the stairs and hit the landing with a noise like an artillery shell.

Standing on the landing and watching this unfold was Comrade who, on seeing a 300kgs bath heading towards him, turned to run. Alas, age, bad diet and a slightly arthritic knee was against him and, as he turned to face his foe and accept his inevitable defeat in escaping the cast iron behemoth, the bath - complete with single mixer tap, shower head and hose, caught up with him and the taps hit him squarely in the testicles.

As if this wasn't injury enough, the shower hose and head became dislodged, reared up like a King Cobra and happy-slapped him round the chops!!!

I would love to say we all rushed to his aide but I'm nothing if not truthful and after watching the bath descend the stairs like it was in the Olympic luge event, and accompanying this with a high pitched "...WHEEEEEEEEEEE!!" we watched it hit him straight in the plums. I'm afraid running anywhere after that was completely out of the question as I was laughing too much. Have you ever seen a grown man cough until his head looks like an aubergine? ... I have.

This was but one of a number of occasions when what outwardly appeared to be a well-planned job turned into a French farce with workmen waving arms, sucking phlegmatically on a roll-up and looking down holes that were either in the wrong place or shouldn't have been there in the first place.

As the months went by, we tried to combine a healthy level of business coming in from Limousin Property Care with renovating our own house and whilst this did take some juggling, on the whole, we managed to make sure that we brought in a bit more than we spent! Work was proceeding at home and we made sure we integrated and ingratiated ourselves with our new neighbours; always there if they needed a hand and, in return, they were always on hand if we needed them.

Chapter 4 - Now That's What I Call a Pile of Gravel

Summer was just arriving. Our neighbours were keen to assist us in the renovation of our house and all of them, naturally, had their own ideas of how this should be achieved. Alas, none of them could come to an agreed plan on a single facet of the renovation and, to a man (and woman), they all had different ideas and different artisans and specialists who, in their opinion, should carry out the work. Whilst all ideas were accepted graciously and were very welcome, most of them were, in truth, worthy of only a moments cursory consideration. Our main source of information was Guy, the maire...or The Oracle as he was known. That was in 2004; nowadays we would call him Siri or Alexa. The house itself, back in the day, had been the main house of a small factory that made sack cloth or hemp. The outbuildings it had on its land were like a treasure trove with bits of old machinery and cloth liberally distributed around the cavernous interiors. It consisted of four bedrooms two larger ones with each hosting a smaller, one presumes, child's bedroom, off of it, access to which was from the upstairs hallway. It also had a large loft that the previous incumbent used to dry washing. Our plan was to convert the loft into two further bedrooms with en-suite bathrooms and use the two smaller bedrooms on the first floor as en-suite bathrooms for the two larger bedrooms.

On the ground floor there was a large kitchen, big enough to use as a kitchen diner and lounge, with a separate dining room opposite the kitchen and off of the main hallway. The house itself was about 150 years old, made in the traditional creusoise style from local granite and with a beautiful flagstone hallway.

Because the house was built with limited but extremely effective foundations, the majority of the house was on bare earth meaning that in winter, when the soil became slightly colder and damp, the hallway flagstones changed colour from light grey to a dark, sombre slate grey that matched the winter skies.

We had always said that part of the process would be for us to carry out as much of the renovation work as humanly possible ourselves so, with this in mind, we made a start. Fortunately, the previous owner was a stonemason, and a good one at that, so the work he had done inside was excellent. Unfortunately, his marriage had broken down irretrievably when he chased his wife around the garden with a shotgun having found out that she was having an affair with his best (soon to become ex-best) friend. That sort of thing doesn't tend to end well in any language or country…all very dramatic and very French.

Guy and Marthe made contact on our behalf with a small, local building company run by two brothers; Fernando and Antoine Simoes.

Trust me, in answer to popular Swedish band Abba's question, no, Fernando never heard a drum; mainly due to fact that his brother never shut up. They were Portuguese by birth but had lived in France for most of their lives. Fernando was quite reserved and just got on with whatever work was required. Antoine on the other hand was a certified lunatic who had an array of different hats depending on his mood, insisted on calling me "Marco" and did impressions of the other artisans on site. I'm pretty sure that in the UK we could have had him sectioned under the 1983 Mental Health Act but in France he was allowed out unsupervised and permitted to use sharp objects and drive large construction machinery. Whilst they were, genetically at least, Portuguese, they had managed to perfect the world renowned 'laisse faire' attitude of the common or garden French artisan through years of dedication and practice.

In France, in order to get an artisan to schedule in your work you sign their quote or 'devis' and from that point, they have 12 months to start the work. Within that 12-month period you are technically required to sit there and wait for them to decide when they fancy starting.

It's a strange old system but it works for them so who am I to judge. The Simoes boys were no different and having signed off all of the necessary documentation we sat back and waited for them to start the work; we waited, and we waited….and we waited.

I'm not saying that promises weren't kept but the last time a signed document was given such little credence and treated with such contempt and impunity in France, they lost the country for six years to Nazi occupation!

It got to about 7 months and I decided to use all of the tact and diplomacy that my parents £5.87 at Swiss finishing school had purchased. I phoned them up and invited them round to look at MORE work. This they readily agreed to do and once inside the house I, to all intents and purposes, locked the door and held them hostage until they told me what time, in what day and, importantly, in what year, they intended to start work. They listened intently as I questioned not only their parentage but indeed whether or not they had the same parents, they put their side of the story as to what was promised, I put mine and, not surprisingly – at least not to me - we decided I was right.

Confident that they would be with us on the 8th September at 8.30 am, as promised, I unlocked the door and let them out. True to their word they turned up on 10th October at midday; I officially gave up.

I am a firm believer that everyone has a talent of some sort. David Beckham had a God given talent for kicking a football better than 99% of the male population which, with a lot of hard work and some fine tuning, turned him into one of the world's best footballers. George Michael wrote one of his first songs aged 17 with Andrew Ridgeley whilst still at school, and whilst on a bus. That song - Careless Whisper - was born of a talent that had laid latent within him and started him on the road to becoming one of the greatest singer/songwriters that ever lived. And let's not forget of course, Gemma Collins…err…well… you get the jist…

Trudy's talent was the ability to look at a building, know EXACTLY what needed to be done, and see the finished article in her mind. Mine was understanding that I was to be seen and not heard when it came to decisions like colours, finishes etc. In short, we made a good team, Trudy told me what she wanted and I told her if it could be done and, if not, why not. Whilst the Simoes boys tackled some of the more specialist work inside, door openings stone pointing and the like, Trudy and I decided to make a start and to put some gravel down outside to tidy up the driveway. After consultation with Guy and Marthe and with the Simoes boys chucking their two ha'pennies worth in for good measure, it was decided we should get the gravel required from the local 'carriere' or quarry.

You can go direct to the source in France, much cheaper and easier to arrange. The only issue was that they tended to be used to dealing with big roadwork companies equivalent in size to the highways departments of a council and they tended to be slightly 'gun ho' when asked to delicately put 1 tonne of gravel in a small trailer.

They took huge delight in dropping it out of the bucket from about 20 feet up and watching as the trailer wheels buckled inwards then outwards and you drove home with a trailer limping along the road looking like Charlie Cairoli's clown car; all four wheels rotating but pointing in different directions. On this occasion however we needed a bit more than one tonne. We didn't know how much exactly but were assured that the operative at the quarry would be able to calculate the volume required for us. Eagerly, and with roughly drawn dimensions in hand, we went to the quarry and, in our broken French, told the man what we wanted. We even took a few morsels of gravel which were the right size with us so that there could be no misunderstanding. The chap looked at the dimensions, scratched his chin (thankfully Trudy was present or the scratching may have extended to other body parts), got his calculator out, banged in some numbers then said "...Quelle epaisseur?" we looked at him blankely…"'ow theeeck? "Ah", I said, "dix centimetres" four inches in old money. He banged a few more numbers into his calculator and said "…quarante deux tonnes" – forty-two tonnes. We agreed the price and arranged delivery. A few days later we heard a rumbling on the road outside.

The lorry carrying our gravel had arrived much to the interest of the neighbours "Zeez inglish. Zay are, 'ow you say, off zere rockers!"

The driver proceeded to deposit the aforementioned 42 tonnes of gravel in the middle of the driveway. He started pouring, and pouring, and pouring. It seemed to be never ending, I'd never seen so much gravel.

All I had to do now was shovel it into a wheel barrow and distribute it over the drive. To put this into context, a fully grown cow weighs about 750kgs so imagine about 56 cows laying on top of each other. One wheelbarrow, full up weighs about 250lbs. I calculated that it would take about 350 wheelbarrows full of gravel…this was a big job.

Our friends Jim and Yvette who we had met on the day we signed for our house, they having signed for their house on the same day, came round to assess the size of the task at hand. They had no intention of helping but liked their schadenfreude served ice cold so revelled in seeing at first hand the job that was more than likely going to kill me. "Wainio boy" - an affectionate term he used from our first meeting and still uses today - "That, my lad, is what I call a pile of gravel...good luck" said Jim, turning on his heels and walking briskly towards the house in case I asked him to help. "Jim" said I, "unless you are going to help, f**k off" a derogatory term I used at Jim on our first meeting, have done so ever since on a regular basis, and have every intention of continuing to do so.

In my opinion, renovating a house successfully, is like wetting yourself when you're wearing a dark suit; you get a nice warm feeling and, afterwards, in return, no-one else notices what you've done. The house started to take shape. There were a couple of unforeseen 'extra' jobs that had to be done; new roof – I'm no expert but when you're laying in bed and getting wet it's either time to strap on an adult nappy or get the roof checked out. Thankfully for all concerned it was the roof that was leaking not my bladder. We had known that the roof would need overhauling, at best, pretty soon, but on closer inspection we were advised that the majority of the roof timbers had seen better days and rather than trying to cut corners, the most cost-effective solution would be to replace the whole thing. This we did and again took advice from the locals on which company to use. Patrick the plumber recommended a local company and this duly went before the committee of neighbours for consideration and verification before we were allowed to phone them. They got the thumbs up or 'pouce leve' as they say in these parts and they arrived a few weeks later. Before Edith Piaf could utter one final *'je ne regrette rien'* the old roof was off, the timbers had been replaced and the new roof was on. All I had to do was rebuild the two chimney stacks that you could see through…again, I'm no expert but never a good sign. This task was made slightly more difficult by the fact that I had an aversion to heights and had never mastered brickwork.

"I can't do that!" I pleaded, "why, are you afraid of heights?" enquired Patrick the plumber "…no, I'm afraid of FALLING from heights" I replied. "…well don't fall off then" said my uncharacteristically understanding wife. After a crash course in staying upright and bricklaying by the previous owner, I managed to rebuild the chimney stacks which to my knowledge, miraculously, are still standing to this day!!

Having only previously tackled renovation work that consisted of things like painting, rubbing down, filling etc, tackling a PROPER renovation job was a bit of a leap of faith in my DIY skills. Over the course of the next 12 months and again in our current house (more of that in the exciting follow up novel: *MARK and TRUDY BUY A DUMP – THE UNNECESSARY*

SEQUEL) these skills were honed to razor sharp. No job was too much (except electrics, water and oil fuelled boiler installation) and we decided that plaster-boarding the kitchen and loft would take priority. Fernando and his psychotic brother had a Portuguese friend who they said would be happy to help with the heavy lifting. This was actually exactly what we needed because, game as she is, lifting a 25kgs sheet of plasterboard up and holding it up to the ceiling was beyond even Trudy's legendary powers. "We'll send him round" they said "his name's Jose". Jose said he would nip over one evening and, surprisingly, he turned up on exactly the right day and at the right time.

He pulled into our driveway, opened the driver's door and got out...and carried on getting out for some time. Jose was the biggest human being I had ever seen...by a long, long way. He sauntered into the kitchen, ducked as he went through the doorway and we thought it best if we turned the lights on as his frame had blocked out the evening sunset. He was huge, 6' 7", and, as he demonstrated, could hold a sheet of plasterboard up to a ceiling with one hand, without a ladder, whilst screwing it in with the other hand. I dropped my voice an octave so that I at least *sounded* more manly than I appeared physically beside this Portuguese colossus.

I looked him up and down – which made my neck crick with the effort – "If he held a light bulb between his teeth, he'd make a marvellous lighthouse!" I whispered to Trudy. Jose was hired (frankly I was afraid to say no...I'd have run away with him and agreed to bear his children if he had demanded so) and together we boarded out the ceiling and filled all the necessary joints ready for finishing. On a side note, Jose's day job was as a *plaquiste* which is someone who plasterboards walls and ceilings and fills the joints ready for the painters to come in to add some colour.

If I thought his plaster-boarding skills were good, I was in for a further shock when I saw him filling the joints! A regular sheet of plasterboard is 250cms x 120cms (8'x4') and filling the joints would mean applying a coat of filler onto each tapered edge and filling the screw holes left when fixing it to the support structure. Having seen him jointing our ceiling, I asked him how much joint work he could do in a day; "un kilometre" he replied – a kilometer...1000 linear metres or 200 boards! The man was a machine...he was also a confirmed wimp as we established when he got a splinter from a fencepost. Still, I wasn't going to be the one to tell him...although I did re-consider my agreement to run off with him and have his children.

Plaster boarding is tough. The sheets are big, cumbersome, heavy and break very easily. After we had completed the kitchen, we decided the next stop would be the loft. The old adage is 'start from the top and work your way down'.

We decided this didn't apply to us but very quickly realised the error of our ways as we found out the hard way that hauling large sheets of fragile plasterboard up two flights of stairs and manoeuvring it into the loft space was tough, dirty, and costly and there were a few casualties along the way. Forty sheets later, and with a pile of plasterboard sheets stacked neatly to avoid damage and also spread the considerable laden weight across the previously untested floor joists, we started the process. I had learned from Jose how to erect the metal framework that the sheets of plaster-board would be attached to and, once this was completed, Trudy and I started the process of attaching the sheets to the ceiling.

From floor level to the roof ridge was about 5 metres and, whilst the sections close to the floor didn't represent a huge physical issue, we needed a plan to get the plaster board sheets up to the top level and up to the ridge. Our plan was to individually take one side of each sheet and simultaneously walk up two sets of carefully positioned ladders.

As I write this, the reality and the stupidity of this plan becomes more apparent. It was an accident waiting to happen…and happen, it did.

As we were fitting one of the sheets near the ridge, Trudy was holding one side of the plaster board sheet and I was stretched up to screw the top row of screws into the sheet and framework beneath. The act of me stretching upwards was just enough to tip the ladder over and this, in turn, made the feet slide across the floor of the loft. The next bit sort of happened in slow motion as I fell, gracefully, from the height of the ridge towards the hard rustic-tiled floor of the loft and I frantically reached out, arms flailing to grab anything that might stop, or at the very least slow down, my descent to floor level. I found something; it was warm and soft and I grabbed on.

Unfortunately, Trudy couldn't support the weight of TWO people on her ladder and the action of me grabbing on to her like duct tape made *her* ladder move and together we fell in unison to the floor, the indignity compounded as a ladder hit me on the back of the head…closely followed by the remains of the sheet of plasterboard.

As luck would have, I landed on the softest part of my anatomy…no, not my head…my backside, which had been liberally upholstered by years of Trudy's excellent home cooking. Trudy was not so fortunate as she landed on her own leg and badly twisted her ankle. To be honest, it could have been a lot worse but, as those of you who have been married for a reasonable amount of time - especially those of the male variety - will know, at certain times, discretion is much the better part of valour because no matter how much trouble you *think* you are in, any form of glib comment at this stage or at times like this can only make it *a lot* worse.

To make things worse…as if that were possible…we were due to go on holiday a few days later to Cavaliere sur Mer on the Mediterranean coast with Jim and Yvette…camping. It's fair to say that Trudy (and myself if truth be told) are, at best, reluctant campers.   I believe a very wise woman (Trudy) once said, and I quote "…*I see absolutely no benefit or point in driving for hours and staying somewhere that is worse than the house you just left…*" This may well be the truest and most accurate assessment of camping I have ever heard and I have no counter argument.

We did go, leaving at some unearthly hour of the morning, Trudy making her way around using a pair of crutches that we managed to acquire from a neighbour before we left. Trudy is not a morning person; in fact, I would go so far as saying the safest course of action is to set two alarms; one to wake her up and another, about an hour later when you are safe to speak to her. Waking her up at 4.30am and bundling her into a car to drive 8 hours to go camping…well…you make your own minds up.

I made a schoolboy error and started speaking pretty much as soon as we got in the car…what was I thinking. She rounded on me like a wounded rhino, extended her neck to its full nine inches and hit me with a tirade of language that almost stripped the skin from my face, followed by *"…STOP – F****NG TALKING YOU ARSEHOLE! ALL YOU DO IS SUCK MY RESOURCES! YOUR'E NOTHING BUT A F****NG LEECH!!!'* Now, I'm no expert, but I appeared to have touched a nerve. I had a feeling her mood wasn't exactly of the 'laisse faire' nature I was used to and if I know one thing, I DO know when it's time to make a strategic retreat. By the time we got to the campsite, her mood had softened slightly…not much but enough to approach under caution and remove the muzzle. We slept on an air bed that slowly deflated each night resulting in us waking up on a rock each morning, got up and got dressed twice a night to have a pee, trudged miserably each morning to join the end of the queue for the communal showers where if you dropped your soap it became impregnated with the discarded DNA of a total stranger, and with which you were then expected to wash your own body, using the hard skin and toe-nail clippings of other campers as an exfoliant. Oh, the unbridled joy of it all. The whole holiday was however made A LOT brighter by Jim nearly drowning at the St Tropez yacht club and Yvette nearly having her International Powerboat licence torn up by a French port authority gendarme, who had the whitest teeth I had ever seen, for speeding in the port.

Cavaliere sur Mer is but a short boat ride to the world-famous St Tropez where we decided to head one day to see what all the fuss was about. Jim and Yvette had a boat – not a huge boat but a lovely 5m speedboat with an inboard motor – which they had towed down to use on the Med. The thought of popping in and out of beautiful coves, being lapped by the beautiful, azure water then spending the evening watching the sunset whilst sipping a glass of chilled white wine on the deck, well, I've got to be honest, did not fill me with dread. It also enabled us to nip across to St Tropez which, surprisingly, was, at one time, a small domestic fishing port and which, even now, still retains some of its original piscary charm. St Tropez has something of a colourful and not entirely uninteresting history. It began life as a very modest fishing village inhabited by the Greeks and then, subsequently the Romans. Legend has it that, in 68 AD, a Roman officer known as Torpes was beheaded on the orders of Emperor Nero. His body (minus his head one presumes) was washed up on the beaches of St. Tropez in a boat, along with a cockerel and a dog. When he was discovered by the villagers, they decided he was a martyr and to adopt him as their patron saint. Every year on the anniversary of his discovery, the locals buy him a hat…just to be ironic. I made that last bit up…not that you'd notice.

The town itself was attacked regularly over the ages, first by the Turks and then by the Spanish, at which point they got a bit fed up with the invading hordes so decided to get some quotes from local builders to build some fortifications. Having come top of the ratings on 'Trustieth thy Trader' and despite not being the cheapest quote, NERO FORTS Ltd EST: 60AD "No job too small, (parva satis ad curam satis magnus ad pluviali/small enough to cope, big enough to care) got the nod and promptly turned up, unloaded the chariots and sent the apprentice off to get 5 cups of meade and some bacon butties. The Citadel still stands to this day. In fact, in 1637 they repelled the Spanish Armada, then towed one of them into the port where they put up a sign next to the local fish and chip shop advertising 'fun day out for all the family including a trip round the harbour, feed the seals, and a 15% discount in the gift shop'.

Despite all of this, it wasn't until the 1920s when St Tropez really hit the big time, with haute couture legends such as Coco Chanel came visiting for their summer 'sojourn' and then in 1954 with the discovery of Brigitte Bardot in the film 'And God Created Women'

On arrival at the port of St Tropez, regulations dictate that, if arriving by boat, you must register your arrival with the harbour master and be allocated a mooring berth. El Capitano Jim duly did this and came back to exclaim that the carpet in the Harbour Master's office was better than he had in his lounge and that we were to move the boat to an available berth alongside one of the other, more regular, residents; a boat called KING.

We found KING quite easily…I say we found it, to be honest it was difficult to miss as it was the size of the Portsmouth/Le Havre ferry and had a 'tender' – a small boat used as a run around when mooring offshore – twice the size of Jim and Yvette's boat called KONG. It had hull fenders covered in suede and on closer inspection we could see two people - the owners we presumed - eating breakfast on deck being fanned by two members of staff. Jim decided that the space allocated to him was not big enough so decided to take action.

"I say…you up there!" he shouted, "be a lamb would you? You couldn't just budge it up a bit could you??"

His request was met with at best indifference and at worst indignance. Safe to say, both KING and KONG remained resolutely moored to the portside and Jim was left looking like a lump of cheese as he attempted to forward and reverse his 5m boat into an impossibly small 15m space.

Nowadays, St Tropez is one of *the* places to be seen for both pretend and actually famous people. It is also very popular with a very diverse range of people who want to be seen and noticed, even if they have done nothing to warrant the attention… Our first experience of this was whilst sipping on a cool beverage in one of the seafront bars, where we were confronted by a man sporting a range of attire that suggested he was either blind or had got dressed during a power cut. He had an overly exaggerated gait with each limb trying to go in different directions, the result of which was that he got nowhere with any great haste and placed in mortal peril, any waiters who came within a metre of him with a fully laden drinks tray.

Putting all of this aside however, the thing that made him stand out from normality was that he was sporting a pair of spectacles with bright red frames but no lenses. He is best described as looking like a Timmy Mallet tribute act. The strange thing is that, in St Tropez, he didn't stand out at all. Everyone was trying to *BE* someone, or at least give the impression that they *were* someone.

Classic case of three cars on the driveway and nothing in the fridge. Nice place but, and I'm sure this will come as a *huge* disappointment to the incumbent residents, Trudy and I have decided that we officially do not want to live there.

Chapter 5 - What Do You Want With Your Ham?

As our business grew, we were fortunate to be able to pick up a number of new customers and one of the 'supply routes' for this were the local estate agents. We made a point in making sure that they became familiar with our company, its services and, with the growing number of brits buying holiday homes in the area, business was good. One of our friends worked at a local estate agent and one day we received a call from her asking if we could meet one of her clients to whom she had sold a property just north of Gueret. We, of course, agreed, and Trudy arrived at the estate agency office at the allotted time. Trudy was immediately introduced to a brother, sister and brother-in-law trio from Yorkshire who were proposing to buy a property in a small, rural, backwater hamlet. It was a bar that had been closed for some time and they wanted to open the doors again and provide the local community with a much-needed resource. *'What's wrong with that?'* the one remaining reader mutters...and this is true, however, they had never seen the bar before; not once. They had seen pictures of the bar on the internet whilst in the UK but had never visited the area, the village or indeed, the property itself. They had owned a couple of pubs near Halifax so the basics of bar work came as no surprise to them. In fact, we learned later that they had intended to move to Spain with some friends to open a pub but the relationship had soured somewhat between Halifax and Calais, and by the time they reached Creuse was fractured beyond repair!

With the other couple heading off to Spain, our trio decided that the apples had fallen far enough from the tree so decided to stop and find somewhere to live on their available budget.

Having seen the bar, the plan was to get it open quite quickly so that the existing licence could be renewed and they didn't need to re-apply for a trading bar licence. In essence we had about a month after the date of completion to decorate the inside and get everything ship shape and ready for *'le grand ouverture'*.

The owners themselves were extraordinary. The brother was as wide as he was tall - and he was quite tall - and could barely walk; although on the upside you could, if required, use his tee-shirt to show a film. His sister wasn't quite the same build but only had one tooth and her main focus and criteria was ensuring that they had Sky TV installed so that she didn't miss an episode of Casualty; in a certain light she looked like a very big bottle opener. Her husband was as skinny as a rake and appeared to be an alcoholic. He had a tight, curly, 'Keeganesque' perm which we discovered during conversation one day, was as a result of falling into the river Nidd in North Yorkshire as a child. He also had a limp which, again, we established, was as a result of falling from a camp bed a couple of years later; one can only assume it was in a tree at the time.

As I pointed out to him though, the glass was half full (in truth more than half full as we were to find out) as between each incident, he had actually had a couple of good years. One would suspect that putting someone of that disposition in charge of a bar was not the greatest plan ever hatched…. In fact, it was probably the worst decision since Herr Hindenburg celebrated the launch of his hydrogen filled balloon by handing out cigars or Klara Hitler's headache subsided enough one evening for her to use all of the latent sexual alure she could muster on husband Alois, and whisper "*Kommen Sie hier meine grosser Liebchen*" in his ear whilst he seized his chance and crossed her normally heavily fortified ramparts with his heavy artillery!

Above all else, their inability to carry out any of the work themselves was overshadowed by the fact that they were completely reliant on other people to speak to the locals and do their bidding for them with any tradesmen. To be fair, the brother, Barry, did at least *try* to communicate with the locals but, alas, with very limited success. His usual victim for his own special brand of French was a young girl who worked at the building supplies company who erroneously, and to her eternal regret, mentioned that she spoke a bit of English.

The conversation generally went something along the lines of…

"Bonjour, oui…morning, morning…Je suis Barry, Bar Entente Cordialle. Je need materials…wood…yes…boize. Combien de wood? 5…grande pieces…mucho longo. Ok…liveraysions…Tuesday…must be Tuesday…neuf o'clock…tres urgent…Wednesday at 4.00 ok…that's fine!

At this point he would put the phone down and declare to anyone that was left listening "Oh yes! I think my French is coming along quite nicely!!"

A project of this size was too big for Trudy and I to achieve within the time frame given, so we enlisted help and once again this was in the form of Jim and Yvette who jumped at the chance to join us on one of our work 'adventures'. By this time, Jim and Yvette were starting on a 2-year career break from the Police force and were happy to pitch in and help us out on anything we thought might be worth doing, and anything that they thought might be a laugh; this was such a project.

The owners had decided on a colour scheme - deep, dark red in case you're interested - and we duly arrived with paint, having used the car as financial security *(paint in France is rubbish and the suppliers charge like wounded rhinos. The only thing that is equally expensive pro rata is cauliflowers…don't even ask)* and all necessary equipment to start on the refurbishment.

In the Police force, Jim and Yvette had positions of some authority, so working with us and being answerable to some of our clients was somewhat of a retrograde step to say the least. The jolly, *joie de vivre* that greeted us when we picked them up, their faces beaming at the thought of the impending adventure, slowly diminished over the course of the day.

The conversation and general banter that had been so evident on the trip *to* the bar had dissipated dramatically by the time we drove home, and was replaced by a reflective, trauma induced silence interspersed only by Jim telling anyone who would listen how he "*…felt like he'd been violated…*" and by Yvette who claimed in another moment of melancholy "*…Normally the only dealings I have with people like that is to arrest them and speak to them when they're under caution …*"

Despite this however, they were nothing if not true to their word and were ready to resume the fight again the following morning. Days at the bar seemed to blur into each other; every day started around the same time and lunch was provided by the owners and always consisted of a ham or meat paste-based sandwich of some description. We asked them once what the meat paste actually was as consuming it left an after taste that I had previously not come across. "Shipman's" they replied, "...what... Harold Shipman?" we retorted. In fact, the recurring presence of ham or Harold's meat paste for lunch was one of the few constants whilst we were there. The other constant was the owners' insistence that Jim's name was actually Richard. No matter how many times we told them "...do you mean Jim?" they would remember for about an hour then revert to asking "...so, what do you think Richard..." at which point we would give up and just carry on calling him Richard until we finished for the day.

So called 'friends' came and went after making the most of the bar's facilities and the owners' hospitality, without so much as picking up a paint brush or indeed paying in most cases, as did artisans and tradesmen who came, saw, and left, never to be seen again. One such regular was a Dutch chap who went by the name of Vim...no surname, just Vim. I fear that confronting a partially French speaking and already confused bar clientelle with an unpronounceable and largely undecipherable Dutch surname might have been the straw that broke the camel's back.

Back in Holland, Vim worked for his local authority project managing major construction projects and, when the patrons announced that they wanted to convert and renovate a barn they also owned, Vim stuck his hand up to manage the project. His first job was to arrange for an architect to draw up the necessary plans which duly arrived a month or so later, only to reveal that where he had drawn on the proposed bedrooms, there was a six metre long and forty-five-centimetre-thick oak support beam. This should have acted as a harbinger of the doom that was to follow but alas no, we just carried on oblivious to the impending carnage.

"OK…" said Vim"…we drink coffee." And drink coffee we did. In a move that surprised absolutely no-one, when we returned to the barn, the beam hadn't moved and was still exactly where the bedrooms were proposed to be. "Ok" said our Dutch foreman, "we will cut it out and put a beam in higher up"

"I'm sure he knows what he's doing" I said to myself "I'm sure that he's done this sort of thing before". I prayed; my face now contorted into a rictus grin as I imagined the consequences of his proposed actions should it all go to shit! A couple of days later, armed with a newly honed chainsaw and having bolted together and positioned two large pieces of Douglas fir higher up the 'A' frame, the moment arrived to cut through the existing main beam.

It was declared by those attending the ritual that I had been designated as the one to be given the honour of cutting through the beam whilst Vim and the other helper stayed on the ground.

"You can stick that honour straight up your arse!" I declared, realising that I would then be held responsible when the front of the barn toppled over into the street. In the end it was the Dutchman's helper who cut through the beam whilst Vim and I slowly retreated towards the door, our ears tuned in like a Doberman for the slightest creak or groan. You could have heard a pin drop.

Amazingly, cutting out the main crossbeam on the 'A' frame did not result in the barn collapsing or any other unforeseen trauma, so the work continued. At no point did the owners set foot in the barn to see how the work was progressing, and by this time, the bar had been refurbished and was open for business.

An average working day was arriving around 8.30 and drinking coffee until Vim decided it was time to start work. This coincided with the owner's sister watching re-runs of CASUALTY re-runs, and the owner himself gracing us with his presence just in time for mid-morning coffee. To be fair, his bedroom was on the first floor and it took him most of the morning to negotiate the quarter turn on the staircase!

A couple of hours and a few *"what do you think Richard?"* later, it was time for lunch, when we played the latest round of everyone's favourite game – 'Sandwich roulette' or 'Baguette bingo' as it was also called.

After lunch I was tasked with returning any phone calls from the morning, despite the fact that the owner's French was, apparently, 'coming along quite nicely' and this was interspersed with the occasional call of "…Mark! French!" at which point, regardless of where I was or what I was doing, I had to hot-foot it to the bar to speak to someone on the telephone.

"Do you know" the owner's sister said to me one day whilst waiting for an update on the condition of her favourite character who had just been admitted to ICU in order for them to try and halt the slow, lingering death of his acting career, "I had no idea I'd have to speak so much French when we moved here". "<u>You</u> don't" I retorted; my tone frosty after being hailed from a ladder to take a call offering cheaper electricity or enquiring if I had been involved in an accident at work that wasn't my fault or did I want to change my mobile phone contract to a worse one for only an extra thousand euros a month.

The work on the bar continued at a pace; the deadline loomed and we simply *had* to get it finished on time. Bedrooms and bathrooms were fitted and it really was a red-letter day when finally, the upstairs shower, available to all three of the owners - not at the same time obviously - was finally installed. "Ooh…I'm so pleased I can finally 'ave a looverly shower…" the owner's sister mused, "up until now it's been strip washes only and quite frankly, I've started to get a bit sore…you know…underneath".

It wasn't so much what she said but the way she cupped her hand and flicked her fingers towards herself in the direction of her lady-garden that made me retch.

Such was her deep involvement in the plot of her favourite soaps, customers were seen more as an annoying interference rather than a source of income and on one such occasion, a local walked into the bar for a mid-morning coffee.

What WAS he thinking? …going into a bar that masqueraded as being open just as a fake plane crashed into the fake Trafford Centre and Charlie had to issue every available ambulance with a 'CODE RED' alert! The offending customer stood at the bar and waited for the bottle opener to get up and serve him…which of course she didn't. Instead, she just sat on the chair that she had positioned strategically in front of the TV and scratched herself on the 'upper, inner thigh' if you get my drift (*N.B for those of you of a nervous disposition, it was the upper inner thigh…for the rest of us, it was her fanny*) whilst shouting up the stairs "GEORGE!!! THERE'S SOMEONE AT T'BAR!!" there was no answer. "GEORGE!!! THERE'S SOMEONE AT T'BAR!!!" still no answer..."GEORGE!!! THERE'S SOMEONE AT T'FRIGGING BA'..." at this point, she was interrupted by a scream down the stairs "FOR FRIGG'S SAKE WOMAN! I'M 'AVIN A SHITE!!!"

...Cue customer turning towards the door and gently closing the door behind them which acted as a precursor for the bottle opener to continue scratching and reverting back to watching Casualty.

A couple of months after starting the barn renovation, we arrived at the bar one day to be met by the owner and his new business partner. An age-old friend from Halifax who used to drink in his pub and who had now agreed to sink every penny he had in the world plus the proceeds of his house and his British Rail pension pot into the bar business. As any normal person would do, having plunged his and his wife's lives into mortal peril, and their life savings and future livelihood into an untried foreign venture, he spent most of the day sitting in the bar reciting George Formby songs. Surely he could see that even if run by a competent individual, the bar was a black hole for anyone's available cash...I'll rephrase that, he was clearly an idiot who couldn't see that the bar – and with it his life savings – was in the hands of three complete incompetents. He didn't bother with unnecessary formalities like getting anything in writing to say that he was part owner, as he had "Barry's word". Consequently, when the funds evaporated, so did his investment and he lost everything.

Our adventure at the bar stopped as quickly as it started. Half way through the renovation work, and whilst clearing the site ready for the next stage, we got raided by the Council's Inspector of Work. He turned up unannounced (obviously… due to the fact that had he announced his arrival, I believe it's called a *meeting* as opposed to a *raid)* and demanded to see the foreman.

The foreman was Vim - the Dutchman - who was noticeable not so much by his absence, but by the sight of him running away down the road closely followed by his assistant. As I was the only one there who was working legally and spoke French…or to be more precise, as I was the only one there, he then demanded to see the owner. I directed him to the bar at which point he turned on the heels of his highly polished shoes and marched up the road clutching his faux leather document bag under one arm, and a ream of papers outlining the 'HIRING OF LABOUR' regulations in the other. On entering the bar, he demanded to see the owner; who did what every self-respecting business owner would do; he hid in the upstairs toilet and refused to come down. This did

NOT go down well with Monsieur l'Inspecteur de Travaux, who promptly issued him with a fine for €30,000!! After appealing the fine (and losing) they paid up; only to be fined a further €20,000 6 months later for hiring illegal workers to replace the barn roof!

At this point we decided that discretion was the better part of valour and declined any further work offered. It had almost reached the point that your reputation was tarnished by association…Tarnished by osmosis.

We did venture back to the bar for a couple of social occasions and on one such occasion we met one of their neighbours who had kindly brought them a basket full of home-grown veg.

The veg in the basket was HUGE! Tomatoes the size of oranges, potatoes the size of melons, carrots as big as a man's calf and a huge array of cucumbers, lettuces, onions. The selection was vast and I asked him where he had his vegetable patch.

"Just round the corner" he replied "would you like to see it?"

"Yes, I would" I said.

We duly set off for the short walk to his allotment. At first sight it was nothing out of the ordinary…a very basic allotment.

"Tell me" I enquired, "what do you put into the ground to make the vegetables grow so large?"

"Absolutely nothing" he replied, "I don't have to"

"Why?" said I,

"...because it used to be a cemetery..."

Our time working at the bar was jam-packed with stories and incidents of which the above are only a selected sample. We could literally fill another book with stories and escapades from our time there.

Generally, I take a light-hearted view and approach to the people we worked with, as they were, ultimately, good people. Yes, they had a slightly skewed approach to how they ran their business but who am I to say this was the wrong approach? They welcomed us in, fed us and paid us on time and for that, we will always be grateful.

Chapter 6 - Gerry and Margot Go To a Barn Dance.

In addition to the work we were doing for clients via Limousin Property Care, we were also working to get the chambre d'hotes up and running. It seemed as though any spare time we had, when we weren't working for other people, we were working on our place…go and live in France they said…you'll have a great time they said…be your own boss, work the hours you want they said… I think that was known as a 'dream de pipe'

Our aim was to get the place finished in time for the summer tourist rush; I say rush…it was more of a leisurely stroll. Our trusty neighbours were there as usual to give advice and they suggested we put up a board on the main road to advertise our B&B. This we did but we were still some ways away from opening our doors to the thronging masses.

In the meantime, and to give us a 'trial run' so to speak of dealing with strangers, we were visited by family – trust me they don't come much stranger – and, on one such occasion, this included a couple who were good friends of Trudy's mum and dad. Gerry and Margot had known Trudy's parents, Eve and Reg for years; Reg had worked with Gerry before retiring, and had invited them to spend a few days with them, visiting us. When they arrived, it became clear that perhaps they had misread the area and the available 'amenities'.

As suitcase after suitcase was removed from the car and the suspension returned to the manufacturers recommended laden weight, the room that Gerry and Margot had been allocated became full with different day and evening wear.

To give you a clue, Creuse is farming belt; if you have two pairs of wellies you get told not to throw your money in people's faces and are considered to be flaunting your wealth. You have a day-to-day boiler suit and one for weekends...that's it...end of. Margot's array of gowns and twin sets which were worn every evening for dinner was, to say the least, a bit over the top. By coincidence, their visit coincided with a 'soiree' at a local bar and restaurant. We had already bought our tickets and enquired as to whether our four guests would like to accompany us. As per normal Jim and Yvette had already said they were coming and we arranged to meet them at the bar, making a grand party of 8 people.

Margot and Gerry excitedly went upstairs to get ready, as did we. I back-combed my eyebrows for the occasion and, when we met downstairs, we were all 'smart casual' except Margot who had gone full

91

Falcon's Crest. Adorned head to toe in a white trouser suit, and with matching necklace and earrings, the conversation stopped as she floated in looking like the love child of 'Priscilla, Queen of the Dessert' and 'Randall and Hopkirk (Deceased). "Blimey Marge" said I, "you do realise you are *in* the Creuse not *on* a cruise don't you?" "Oh this old thing?" Margot enquired "Just something I threw on" and with that exited stage left. We all hurriedly followed her and off we set.

The bar itself was a typical Creusoise establishment. Minimalist and decorated in a style circa 1975 by someone who was evidently colour blind. The walls were adorned with hand painted images of the Amazon jungle, complete with monkeys, crocodiles and palm trees on two of the walls and roughly painted pictures of what I think was ancient Egypt on the other two walls *(I couldn't be 100% certain but there was a bloke in a skirt with a squint in one eye standing in a portico and a pyramid that had a door in it. To be honest your guess is as good as mine).*

I had sat myself next to Jim and we were behaving like two naughty schoolboys; well, he was, I just followed his lead. Not much of a defence I grant you but it's the only one I've got and on that note Your Honour, the defence rests. The food was edible if a little sparce but considering it was only just edible, its meagre presence was somewhat of a godsend. "Well," said

Jim "the food might be shit but you've got to go a long way to beat the view!"

The entertainment for the evening was provided by a musical duo...let me rephrase that...by two blokes who had a rough idea of what they *wanted* to play but had no real idea of exactly *how* to play it. The drummer was wearing a denim boiler suit and his drum kit consisted of a snare drum and a set of 'top hat' cymbals. The pianist was obviously the 'eye candy' of the outfit as he could walk unassisted and had on a pair of black leather trousers that were so tight, I could count the change in his front pocket; €1.85 in case you're interested plus a Topic...at least I think it was a Topic. He was mincing around the dance floor in black Cuban heeled cowboy boots, like a vision on Voltarol.

He really did make a mockery of his 85 years and, as Ginger Baker belted out a back beat on his drums, the Creuse's answer to Jerry Lee Lewis brought the act to a crescendo by adorning an array of rubber masks whilst assaulting the audience with a cacophony of notes from his piano, none of which sounded anything like any song by anyone, ever.

Margot's face looked like she'd been dipped in a bucket of iced water and tasered. Have you ever seen anyone's facial muscles pull their hair back over their head? I have. Her evening was made complete when the pianist came over to her, held his hand out and requested her presence on the dance floor. Jim and I giggled.

He seemed rather insistent and, for a moment, I thought she was going to oblige. As she stood next to him, with him dressed entirely in black and her looking like the ghost of Christmas past, it looked like a TV where the horizontal hold had gone funny. She looked a picture as she got up to what everyone assumed was to join him on the dance floor. As she ran past him, just for a split second, it looked like a giant mint humbug had taken centre stage, like a bar code. But it wasn't to be as she hastily ran to the exit doors and sanctity of the ladies' loos.

She did come back to her seat, but not for a while. I think she wanted to wait for the hullabaloo - some might say brouhaha - to die down. In her defence, with him running around like a geriatric lunatic ripping rubber masks on and off with alacrity, a girl doesn't know where she stands does she? To be fair, her other half, Gerry, was no use at all and just sat there laughing as poor ol' Margot got both barrels and unwittingly turned into the evening's star attraction.

As the year passed by, we were frequented by both family and friends. It was good to see them; would have been so much better if they'd paid but hey ho!

As much as we were enjoying our new lives, it was nice to see familiar faces, share some memories and laugh about some of the things that had happened to us in the short time we had been in France.

Earlier in the year we had acquired a puppy, Ben. He was a golden cocker spaniel and, little did I know at the time, he would be the best friend a man could wish for. He was my first dog and the bond between us grew and got stronger with every day. He was like my shadow and followed me wherever I went. If I went to work, he wanted to come with me. If I was mowing the lawn, he wanted to sit on the ride-on mower with me. If I had decided to sit under a tree for six hours, Benny-boy would have been happy just to sit there with me. I loved him, and he loved me back...unconditionally. When he died suddenly aged 13 in 2016, I was heartbroken...when I think of him, I still am. We have two other cocker spaniels now; Holly who grew up with Ben and, at the time of writing, is now aged 13 herself, and Phoebe aged 3...and a little rascal. I love them both but my bond with Ben was unshakeable and unbreakable; I still miss him and think of him every day.

Back then, early September came and with it, a visit from my sister and brother-in-law. They arrived about a week after my birthday and it gave me the chance to try out a present I had received from my In-Laws...A metal detector. My brother-in-law, Graham, by general consent backed up by years of proof, is an accident waiting to happen.

As an example, I firmly believe he is the only human being - ever - to be painting a ceiling, step down the ladder and put his foot into the tray of dark paint, then walk over the light-coloured carpet and into the kitchen to tell my sister what had happened. We would all like to do something heroic in our lives; Graham has more chance of tripping over his cat and cutting his head open on a tube of Smarties.

As we had a reasonably big garden, it seemed like the perfect place to start. I enlisted Graham's help in assembling the equipment and together we went outside like excited schoolchildren to start running the metal detector over the garden to see what hidden treasures we could uncover. I gave Graham a small hand shovel and, armed to the teeth, and confident he couldn't cut his own leg off, I took one step forward with Graham in tow. I had only gone a couple of metres, frantically sweeping the metal detector from side to side, when it beeped.

I narrowed it down to an area the size of a saucer, and shouted to Graham "Graham! Dig my spade laden amigo! Dig like you've never dug before!" Graham started digging for his life and it wasn't long before we had a hole in the ground about 6" wide by about 8" deep. Alas, nothing. I continued walking and again, after a couple of metres, the detector beeped again. Again, I commanded Graham to dig for his life and he duly obliged. Again, nothing. This set the scene for the next two hours; me walking, every two metres the machine beeping and Graham digging like his life depended on it.

Alas, with every bleep and with every hole, the result was the same; nothing. Unsurprisingly, by the time we had covered most of the garden, Graham had a bit of a sweat on.

It was about 85 degrees and the effort of digging had reduced him to a wizened husk; he looked like an unwrapped Pharoah. It was then that I realised why our efforts had resulted in nothing. No buried treasure, no hoard of roman coins...nothing.

When we came out to start our treasure hunt, I had put on my gardening boots...my gardening boots that had metal toe caps. Every beep the detector had made was as it passed my feet and picked up the metal caps in my boots.

As I looked over the garden and surveyed the asymmetrical pattern of a hundred or so holes in the lawn I turned to Graham and decided to deflect the blame. "Trudy's not going to be happy with you me ol' son" I said "...what *were* you thinking?"

He trudged back to the house with me for a beer
"...stupid boy..." I muttered.

Chapter 7 - Our First Guests

As we contemplated life in the hospitality sector, thoughts turned to the B&B and getting it ready for paying guests. Freeloaders were banned unconditionally and, anyway, Ben didn't really have a lot of time for strangers so that was good enough for us. By that time, we had acquired a sister for Ben – Holly (see previous chapter) – who loved him like a big brother and who he tolerated like an annoying itch. Being a *working* cocker as opposed to a *show* cocker, she was as different to Ben as it was possible to be whilst still being the same breed. Ben's idea of exercise was to sit on his chair - yes, he had his own chair - whilst sipping a glass of claret and watch people walk down the road. Holly's idea of exercise was a sprightly 5-mile run, then chase as many pheasants as possible whilst watching us run across fields to stop her, then run off just as you got to her and go back home, sleep for about half an hour and expect to do it all again. Her nicknames of 'Paula Radcliffe' 'The Black Flash' and 'The Pocket Rocket' were not given out lightly and without good reason.

Our neighbours continued to engage us in conversation and enquire how the renovation work was progressing and we dutifully replied that it was progressing on schedule. One evening there was a knock on the door and the Maire's wife stood there.

She asked us if we were open for paying customers. "…that depends" I said, we HAD a bedroom but it was a long way from finished and had a hole in the ceiling.

"…These poor people have been travelling all day and just need a bed for the night and something to eat" she said "well we have a barn if the room's no good!" said I, "It used to be a stable…and it's a lovely clear night; look at the size of that star overhead!"

I was sure I'd heard that story before somewhere but couldn't place it exactly.

It transpired that the people concerned were Russian. She was as thin as a rake with unnaturally blond hair and a slightly fixed expression on her face. She didn't say a word for the duration of their stay. He, on the other hand, was more garrulous and spoke perfect French which we discovered later on, he learned from watching French TV in Russia…all the rage apparently. He was the Communications Director for a famous Russian football club and he told us they came to France for their annual holidays every year. Trudy and I showed them to the building site that was masquerading as their room, and left them to make themselves at home. Trudy was in panic mode. The arrangement was for a room AND a meal but, being unprepared for their arrival, we had no meal prepared and it was going to have to be 'off the hoof'.

I decided the best way forward was subterfuge, my plan being that if we sat them outside - perfectly acceptable on a warm summer's evening - and put on just the bare minimum of *VERY* ambient lighting, it would capture the romance of the evening whilst at the same time, pretty much rule out their chances of actually seeing what they were eating.

We went from having 'nothing in that was suitable' to Trudy rustling up and presenting a feast of a dinner with cheese, wine and dessert that was, according to our guests, "…a triumph!!"

They retired to their room replete and with a smile on their face that only young love can bring; either that or she had got too near the candle and her botox was melting.

The following day they arose promptly and came down for breakfast. I asked the chap if they had slept well. "Comme les anges" he replied…'Like the angels'; either that or it was "comme le sange" which is 'like a monkey' although whilst not being particularly conversant with the sleeping habits of primates other than my friend Barry – that seemed unlikely. It was a very poetic end to a slightly fraught evening but they paid, thanked us for our hospitality and were soon on their way. We had 'cassé'd our canard'

Our 'canard' was 'cassé'd a few times after that whilst we were doing work on the house.

Most people left having been fed, watered and having had a comfy bed for the night and it brought in a few quid to help us along the way. There really is nothing like looking up at the stars and listening to the crickets 'chirripping' under the moonlight to get you off to a dream filled, restful sleep; admittedly it did come as a surprise to a few of the guests when it became apparent they would be doing that whilst lying in bed via the hole in their ceiling but everyone enjoyed it and I like to think it added to the holiday experience.

I was very much 'front of house' on the basis that I had no culinary skills but did have the ability to carry plates and make general chit-chat with the guests whilst Trudy was in the engine room making a four-course meal - and wine - from a tomato and a carpet tile. It seemed to work well as the property market in UK was booming and many of the guests that we had were looking for holiday homes of one sort or another. It also gave me the chance to slither my way into their good books like a greasy old rag and offer them the benefit of my extensive knowledge and expertise as a European landowner. I wasted no time in promoting our services - which many of the poor unsuspecting souls gratefully accepted - and who are still customers to this day. Trudy often said she often felt a bit sorry for our guests as I primed them up with seemingly innocent questions, then locked the dining room door and talked them into submission and refused to let them out until they signed on the dotted line for work of one sort or another. I think that was a bit harsh…we didn't have a lock on the dining room door.

The array of guests we encountered whist in the hospitality sector was vast. We had guests from Australia, Holland, Belgium, Russia, UK and from just about every region in France. From holiday makers and house hunters to about-to-be-weds and illicit lovers, we had them all. With each booking came a frisson of excitement as they pulled up and disembarked and we peeked around the curtains to see what they looked like and whether or not they matched or come close to matching the images we had conjured up in our minds of how they would look.

Of course, there were always the 'curve-ball clients' who hadn't pre-booked but saw the chambres de hotes signs on the main road and made a last-minute decision to stop for the night. You didn't know what you were getting when they knocked on the door.

One such encounter was a couple who turned up one afternoon whilst I was at work. They had, apparently, seen the signs on the main road and needed a room for the night. Trudy, courteous and amenable as ever showed them to their room and left them to settle in. The woman was *heavily* pregnant and, having left them to unpack, Trudy had gone back into our part of the house that was off-limits to customers.

Shortly afterwards, the man came down to explain to Trudy that there was no hot water. Trudy was perplexed but went upstairs to their room to try and ascertain the problem. As she turned the tap on, the hot water came out as normal and after offering an apology, Trudy went back downstairs again to carry on with whatever she had been doing. A few minutes later, the couple came back downstairs and explained that they were going into the local village to get some cash and, with that, jumped in their car and sped off.

Trudy smelt a rat. As they span the wheels and the car lurched forward and out of the drive, she quickly noted down their car registration number. She then went back up to the room and did a slightly more than cursory check of the bits and pieces that had been there. All seemed in order and she then went back downstairs whereupon she noticed that her purse had gone. It had been stolen. Clearly the nefarious duo had a well-oiled plan under these circumstances whereby when the proprietor went up to deal with the false claim of no hot water, the female member of the duo, who had secreted herself out of eye shot, would go into the proprietor's vacated area and search for valuables, money and such like.

When I came home there was a gendarmerie car parked outside which did sharpen my focus a bit and, when I went in, the entire sorry episode was explained to me. The gendarmes were brilliant and said they would keep us informed which they did and, about six weeks later, they reported to us that they had apprehended the couple as they drove through a motorway toll-booth. They also told us that the male had been arrested for other 'more serious' offences.

About two months after their capture, I had a call from the local gendarmerie to say that they had received a letter for us, from the woman, and would I come down to the gendarmerie. I went along and they gave me the letter which was a long, arduous narrative about how the man had 'made her do it' and how she 'wasn't a bad person' and she enclosed €20.00 as recompense for the money they had taken and asked me for forgiveness. What was that I could hear? Was it the plaintive sound of a barrel being scraped and her lawyer vainly clutching at a collection of straws as he or she highlighted to the court how their client was a 'changed person' and that this was a 'momentary lapse' and not to be repeated?

I read the entire letter then explained to the gendarme that €20.00 was only about half of the entire sum of cash that had been in Trudy's purse so she wasn't THAT sorry and that he was welcome to put this in their own benevolent fund. I asked him, if I did a reply, would it be read out in court as part of a victim statement. He wasn't sure but we thought I should give it a go anyway.

He fettled around for a pen and paper and, as I stood to my full 5'11" and said "take this down my good man!", he licked the end of his pencil and clamped his tongue between his teeth as he studiously wrote down everything I said.

I told her that she was stupid and therefore a victim of her own stupidity. She was rotten to the core and I certainly did NOT forgive her for what she did. As far as I was concerned, she could wallow in her own self-pity whilst in prison; and, by the way, I sincerely hoped that any sentence she was given would give her ample time to reflect on the trauma she had caused my wife and how she would feel if she had been the victim of a similar crime.

I also proclaimed, using both a pointy finger AND wavey arms, as I paced up and down the gendarmerie office (for I was in full flow now and, as cricket lovers among you will understand, 'coming off my long run'), that it was of great solace to me that the vast majority of French people were honest, decent, hard-working people who found crimes of her sort abhorrent and that she should be thoroughly ashamed of herself. I mean, could she imagine the outcry if it ever got out that we had no hot water? What I really wanted to say was that she was a rotten, thieving slag who could stick her €20.00 up her Gaelic arsehole but, alas, my vocabulary and phraseology were hindered by the fact that I was only on CD 4 of the 'MICHEL THOMAS TEACH YOURSELF FRENCH FOR BEGINNERS' course.

The gendarme laughed…and popped the €20.00 note into the station biscuit fund.

I think we both *really* hoped they *did* read it out in court. I like to think they did, and they both got porridge.

Chapter 8 - Germans Fawlty

What do these people have in common? You can have as many guesses as you want...**Hazel Brugger, Jan Böhmermann, Bülent Ceylan, Enissa Amani, Olaf Schubert, Henning Wehn.**

The answer is, they are, according to some people, a rare breed. They are all successful German stand-up comedians. There are few nationalities in the world that have a sense of humour like the Germans; let me put that another way, most nationalities in the world *have* a sense of humour...except the Germans. Ok so Henning Wehn might have given it away and, in truth is one of the funniest comedians I've heard but, in general, let's be honest, they are not known for their riotous, hilarious comedy sketches. Beer, fast cars, unregulated motorway speeds, efficiency? Yes...by the bucket load...but, by general consensus, they ain't for larfs!

However, I must say, I would disagree. One of the funniest couples we had to stay in our chambre d'hotes were German; and not only German, but of a type of German that would have made makers of stereotypes point and say "...Look! German!" Blond herr ...sorry... hair, tall athletic; the man was a Teutonic masterpiece. They spoke English - of course they did, why wouldn't they - they said they would arrive at 4.30pm and at 4.32 they knocked and the door and couldn't stop apologising for their tardiness.

Now I have, for some time, believed that any song ever written, if sung in a German *'allo 'allo* type accent is immediately improved…try it…pick a song, any song, and sing it in a German accent. See? better isn't it?

When they arrived – for the sake of the story we shall call him the Kaiser – the Kaiser greeted us with a hearty "HELLO!!! I am ze Kaiser, but my friends call me…vell… Kaiser actually!". I was immediately intimidated. Mr and Mrs Kaiser followed us up to their allotted room and I feared it may be the last time we were in control of the situation or indeed allowed to do anything of our own free will until *they* decided we could. The temptation to put on marching band oompah music was almost overwhelming but I managed to control myself and refrain from anything contentious; I did mention my grandmother was from Poland once but that was about as close as I got. They had booked for a week but, as Holland and France found out between 1939 and 1945, once they were there you had a devil's own job to get rid of them. They seemed OK however, and we left them to unpack and settle in. No sooner had Herr and Frau Kaiser arrived, than they had donned their walking boots, strapped on their backpacks and disappeared out the front door. They returned a few hours later and went and sat in the garden with their backs to the wall under the wisteria; basically, they had formed a beachhead where they could see any advancing guests.

Being 'front of house', it was my job to approach tentatively and see if they required any form of refreshment. I collaborated, they discussed it and replied in the affirmative...at least I think they did...difficult to tell really as whenever German people talk to each other it doesn't matter what they say it always sounds as though they're about to invade somewhere. When I returned, they beckoned me to sit down...I say beckoned...

"Pleeze...*SIT*!" I sat as instructed. "ve vant to explore ze sur-r-r-ounding area oont do not have ein map. Might ve tr-r-r-rrruble you for a 1-500 scale map pleeze? I gave them the only map I had and they looked at it with slight disdain.

"vell, itz not perfekt but vot kan you do? HA HA HA!!"

I laughed – nervously. With that I gave them their drinks and as soon as it felt safe to do so made my escape. Just to be on the safe side I walked in a zig-zag fashion away from them in case they were lining me up in their crosshairs.

The following morning, they came down (looking immaculate I might add as only Europeans seem able to do so) and tucked into their breakfast of fresh French bread, warm croissants, cereal, fruit, yoghurts and coffee, before bidding us a cheery "GOOTBYE!", jumped in their car and off they went. We both breathed a small sigh of relief as we saw them disappear up the road and settled in to our daily routine.

They returned mid-afternoon carrying a couple of bags. We were in our kitchen – the only part of the entire 4 bedroomed house, other than our bedroom that we could say was truly ours. The rest of the house was given over to the chambre d'hotes.

We saw them get out of the car and then, to our surprise, there was a knock on the kitchen door.

"…Gut afternoon!!!" said the Kaiser "Vood it be possible to put some items in ze fridge?"

" Vot…sorry, what items?" I enquired.

"Some cheez oont some garlic liver sausage," said Herr Kaiser

The man was turning into a parody of himself.

"Yes OK" I replied

"ve vill have zem for br-r-r-eakfast viz ze coffee" "Schnooki my vife is not so keen on ze pastries…zey make her feel...vot is ze vord...bloaty...I know...vot can I tell you"

Sure enough, the following morning we heard them come downstairs at which point the kitchen door flew open and the Kaiser marched in and strode intently up to the fridge, with the look of a man on a mission of some sort.

"Sorry, can I help you at all? Said Trudy, brandishing a large bread knife.

"ah yes Madame Vain! Guten morgen, I voz looking for ze sausage oont ze cheez"

"well you go and sit down and I will bring them to YOU" said Trudy, pointing the kitchen knife in his direction.

"oh jah, jah" said the Kaiser and he beat a negotiated retreat into the dining room.

Once there, they sat at their usual table and I brought him his cheese and his garlic sausage, a sharp knife, two plates and some French bread and left them to it.

I went back in about 10 minutes later to find him having spread a large ordinance survey map across the table (much to the chagrin of the French couple who were having breakfast at the table at the time) with him and his wife marking out villages and towns on the map with a black felt tip pen.

It looked like they were planning another invasion so I cocked an ear in case any intel came my way that resistance forces might find useful.

There was nothing that would have been of interest, unless of course their planned lunch restaurant turned out to be of strategic importance, but what WAS of interest was the fact the Kaiser was using the sharp knife to eviscerate the cheese and garlic sausage, not on the plate, but on Trudy's pristine damask tablecloth.

I wasn't sure how to break the news to Trudy about his mis-demeanour. I felt sure he would try and weasel his way out of it by claiming he was only following hors d'ouevres… sorry…orders. Trudy was VERY protective of her tableware and having it treated like this was going to hurt - him not her. I made sure she wasn't in reach of any sharp or pointed items before I told her, after which she marched in to the dining room, grabbed his garlic sausage – (*Ed. oh come on, you're better than that!*) - and slammed it down on the plate before turning a full 180 degrees and marching back out. Clearly it was my fault so I had what is known in our house as the 'broken telly' routine – no picture or sound – for a couple of hours before she calmed down again.

Again, they came back around mid-afternoon and, again, there was a very efficient, well-practiced and intimidating *'Rat-a tat-tat'* on the kitchen door. This time, I was ready for him. I threw the door open and caught him just as he was about to go for a second round of rat-a tat-tatting.

"Gut afternoon Mister Vain" "Ve are considering staying oont eating here for ze dinner tonight, could you oblige and tell me vot iz on ze menu"

I looked at Trudy who was making faces at him from the safety of the far end of the kitchen and trying to teach Ben to goosestep.

"Salmon" she said

"Salmon" I said

"Aah Ok...I vill check viz my vife...she's not so keen on ze seafood".

About a quarter of an hour later I heard him marching briskly and efficiently up the hallway and he knocked on the kitchen door. I opened it; similarly briskly and similarly efficiently. He stood there and clicked his heels together...no he really did!!

"Gut news Mister Vain! Ve vill accept ze salmon !!"

"I vil alert ze media" I replied.

Mr and Mrs Kaiser were very accommodating and allowed us to do whatever we wanted whilst they were out. The cheese and liver sausage were consumed with monotonous regularity every morning and left a garlic fog in the dining room like a meaty Chanel No 5 that imparted a glazed look on Ben's face as he searched in vain for the source. I'm not sure which area of Germany they came from; frankly I was afraid to ask in case I slipped up and gave away crucial information under pressure...loose lips and all that.

I imagined they lived in a Bavarian castle like the King and Queen in Chitty Chitty Bang Bang with servants and children working for them in sub-terraneous talcum powder mines...Ok maybe not. After a couple of days, we had started to share a couple of jokes with them - none about the war – based primarily around other nations that one or the other of our countries had invaded at some point in history.

By the time they left we had whipped them into shape and they had started to behave like proper people - not savages - in the dining room. There was the occasional 'faux pas' but a quick 'crack' round the back of the head with a table mat or a flick from a rolled up napkin soon reminded them of the error of their ways. I also made it abundantly clear that using Trudy's damask table linen as a cutting board was strictly *verboten* and, if this was repeated, for him and his frau, it was most definitely *'gute nacht Vienna'*.

I kept my eyes and ears open over the course of the subsequent few days; just in case they announced that the Alsace or any other regions had been annexed...again... but nothing ensued and eventually we reduced the war footing to orange.

As guests go, they were perfect. They arrived on time, went out soon after, kept their room in immaculate condition, paid and went home...If only all of our guests had been like that...

Chapter 9 - Vlad the Impaler

They say opposites attract. Donald and Ivana for example, Julia Roberts and Lyle Lovett, that dog on the internet who is now life-long buddies with an orphaned duck, the list goes on. We did have some quirky, sometimes odd, sometimes downright weird guests in the chambre d'hotes; we even had Australians at one point.

One such couple booked up for a week's stay and, as was the normal procedure, we sent them details of our address and a route of how to get to us. Where we lived was about 7 hours from Calais so generally people would arrive late afternoon or early evening after making the trip across on either ferry or tunnel. If we knew people were on their way, we would keep an eye out or an ear cocked for the phone or a strange car meandering through the village with waifs and strays aboard.

Outside the front door we had a small brass bell; the type that normally has TITANIC written on it on one side and MADE IN CHINA on the other. It made it easier to hear if you were strolling around the grounds or checking the East wing. About 7.00pm we were taking advantage of a cold beverage in the evening sun and playing the usual game of 'Guess the Guest'

…you know the one, it's the game where you try and form a mental image of the person on the other end of the phone then see how close you are. Trudy was particularly adept at this and was in the last of the Champion's League spots with a game in hand…when there was a very feint 'ding…ding…' from outside the front door.

I bounded to the door full of vim and vigour and threw the door open. "HELLO!" I said enthusiastically as the door went back on its hinges.

"…hello…" whispered the small, unnaturally pale man with ridiculously unkempt hair who had been standing on the doorstep, but who had taken a leap backwards when I burst through the front door and he thought I was going to attack him.

"My name's Brian"

"Mark" I replied

"No, Brian" he said.

"No, *I'm* mark" I answered, this time in a more softly spoken, gentile fashion. He looked like the sort of bloke who worked in IT, never saw daylight and had eyes like a bush baby. "Sorry, I didn't see you down there…let me help you up…oh, you are up…Ok, apologies."

"I'm Brian" said Brian.

"Yes I know...you just told me that. Shall we start again?"

It was going to be a long night and an even longer week I suspected.

Brian went back to get his luggage and it was at this point the passenger door of his car flew open and I was confronted by his other half, a slim oriental looking woman whose voice made milk curdle and the windows rattle in their frames. Her voice was one thing but her most outstanding feature was her teeth.

She looked like she'd swallowed a handful of javelins. It wasn't just the size of her teeth - HUGE - or the amount she was carrying around - as a conservative estimate I would say there was at least two pianos - but it was the angle at which they were protruding; they stuck out at 45 degrees to her mouth. She could have eaten both sides of an apple at the same time.

"HERRO" she said "my name Su Li"

She had a very thick accent and that, coupled with the mouthful of cutlery she appeared to be chewing, made her very difficult to understand.

"Ten to eight" I said...deciding the best course of action was to have a punt at what she said in the absence of any decipherable words.

"NO! ME..SU LI" she screeched.

119

I paused for a moment, initially to wipe the blood from my ears but also to give myself some thinking time. 'OK' I considered 'so it's nothing to do with the time and she did have her hand held out so it must be something to do with her name'.

"Hello Su – I'm Mark"

"Dis luvvery prace you got! She added

"Thanks" I said "shall we go inside?"

Brian had already gone in and we followed suit. I showed them up to their room and we walked past the kitchen where Trudy was preparing the meal that they had requested for that evening.

I left them to settle in and went back downstairs. Trudy was busy in the kitchen and when I walked in, she asked me what they were like.

"Well, he's virtually silent and she screams like a banshee" "She's what I would describe as Amazonian."

"What, 6 feet tall, broad shoulders and looks like Xena Warrior Princess?" said Trudy

"No, I think he ordered her on the internet and she was delivered next day by courier". "No returns label on her though as far as I can make out so might be tricky if he wants to send her back".

That night, we waited for Brian and Su Li – now affectionately called Vlad the Impaler – to come down for dinner; predominately because Trudy said that I *must* have over exaggerated her appearance. Fifteen minutes later and her apologies had been accepted. My brief synopsis had been unerringly accurate. They were very pleasant; Brian said nothing and Vlad was very chatty throughout. A more diametrically opposed couple it would be hard to find.

As hors d'ouevres were finished, I went in to collect their plates. Su Li beckoned me over…

"Hoo wu foboh?"

"What??" I said vehemently racking my brain for the Cantonese of 'that was delicious'

"Hoo wu foboh? You know foboh today" and with that made a kicking action.

"Oh! Who won the football!!!"

At the time of their arrival, it was the 2008 European Championships and Vlad was clearly a fan. I went through the day's results, she cheered at some and winced at others, and then her concentration went back to her dinner as Brian carefully sharpened her front incisors ready for the next course…after all, he was nearer to them than she was.

One of the positive aspects of eating with us was free wine; after all, wine was cheaper as water. Guests would have a four-course meal including cheese and coffee and as much wine as they could drink. Normally people knew when to reign it in a bit but there were always the odd one or two, normally Brits…let me rephrase that…always Brits, who had no 'off 'button and they were treated accordingly and sent packing.

The rules according to Gites de France, who lay down the chambre d'hotes gradings and regulations, state that the host or hosts were supposed to eat *with* the guests but this never happened on the grounds that we ate around 7.30 whereas the guests would generally eat later than that, normally having been out and about all day, and it seemed churlish to put a curfew on them simply because we wanted to eat.

That evening, Brian and Vlad were the only guests 'eating in' and they tucked in vociferously. After they had finished the meal and we'd wiped the gravy off of the walls, we offered them an after-dinner snifter. Brian declined announcing "No, I think we've had enough". The disappointment on Vlad's face was palpable and she announced *"I would rike annuver grass of wine!"*

Brian looked at her and I could see he wasn't happy. His neck and face turned purple as his rage grew.

He was incandescent with rage as he spat through gritted teeth at Vlad *"I said, we've... had... ENOUGH!!!"*. She cowered back down as he announced "I think it's time we went to bed!".

Su Li dutifully followed him as he rose to his full 5'4" and strode purposefully out of the dining room and up the stairs to their room. I felt slightly guilty that I had unintentionally stumbled into a personal moment and felt the only way to exorcise this was to tell Trudy what had happened. I told her how Brian had released his inner chimp (*see THE CHIMP PARADOX by Prof Steve Peters) "ooh" she said, "sounds like he needs a slap" It would take a REAL man to stop Trudy having a drink if she wanted one; and a real BIG one at that.

Breakfast was normally served from 8.00am until 10.00 am; it gave the guests the chance to have a bit of an easy start to the day and still allowed us to get on with whatever the day had in store for us.

After the previous evening's events, I was slightly uneasy at what the morning might bring. At about 8.05, We heard Brian and Su Li come downstairs and go into the dining room. As was my job, I went in to bid them "good morning" and offer a generic "did you sleep well? Would you like tea or coffee?". Years of practice had made me sound almost sincere when asking this, whereas the truth was as long as *we* got a good night's sleep that was all I worried about. A bit like asking someone 'how are you?', you do it out of courtesy; you don't actually expect them to give you their potted medical history do you?

It was a strange sight that I was confronted with. Both Brian and Vlad were sitting at the dining room table looking very much worse for wear, Brian's hair was even more unruly than the previous day and they were both in their pyjamas. I'll be honest, it took me back slightly. Well, you don't expect it do you? They mumbled something about coffee and I made my exit. Having made the coffee, I returned to the dining room, tray in hand, and was confronted by them both sitting upright, spoons in hand…fast asleep.

I mean, the whole idea of having a two-hour window for breakfast was so that you could, if you wanted, have a lay in. It was a chambre d'hotes not a gulag. So, with that in mind, what's the point in getting up early when you don't have to? I know the breakfasts were nice but they weren't THAT great!

I made a point of dropping some cutlery on the tiled floor just to see them levitate out of their seats: Brian went a step further and sprayed himself with milk and Cocoa Pops. I felt a certain sense of satisfaction when he did it and I sniggered childishly. "Oh sorry…I didn't mean to interrupt" I said, lying through my teeth. Good job I wasn't lying through HER teeth or it would have been the biggest lie ever told. "Can I get you anything? More coffee? More bread? Tungsten tips for your javelins?

All of my suggestions and offerings were politely declined and they hurriedly finished their breakfast and scampered off upstairs to ready themselves for their day's adventures.

This routine was followed with almost religious fervour for each morning of their stay; down at 8.02, fully adorned in their pyjamas, dishevelled appearance, quick kip at the breakfast table then back upstairs about 8.30, not a word spoken in the interim and then out.

I got the distinct impression that Vlad just did what Brian wanted and, with that in mind, every day we waited for them to depart before going up to tidy their room, fully expecting to see a note secreted somewhere declaring that she had been kidnapped and asking us to alert the authorities.

Their departure was as curious as their arrival. Su Li smiling, the sun reflecting off of her front canines and nearly burning our retinas out as she gave us a cheery wave and headed for the car, Brian already in the driving seat staring downwards to avoid eye contact and talking to us whilst staring down at the clutch pedal. We didn't hear from them again.

I wondered sometimes whilst sucking on a thoughtful tooth if they were still together or if Su Li had started an escape committee and made it to the compound fence while Brian slept in front of his PC…who knows, they might have been perfectly happy together, or, alternatively, she might have picked her moment and spun her head round suddenly, slitting his throat with her finely honed incisors like a sabre-toothed Samurai assassin as he slept.

Chapter 10 - The Curious Case of the Frozen Fish

Our neighbours at Grand Villard were a curious collection of individuals, from very different walks of life.

Within the village we had, at any one point, people whose skills came from a number of different trades and industries; draughtsman, plumber, dentist, accountant, artist (painter), nurse, social care worker and doctor living alongside the likes of farmers, hunters and us, ex-salesman with 20 years' service in a suit and an ex-receptionist at a Japanese bank. It made for a diverse mix, and that's without taking into account that two of the couples were in same-sex relationships; very un-Creusoise in the machismo society that much of France operates under. But French people are nothing if not accepting of diversity and the 'laisse faire' attitude for which France is known around the world meant that all types, colours, creeds and orientations were given a hearty 'Bienvenu' into village life…except the bloke who lived on the edge of the village who was a dark, bleak soul and a bit of a nutter if truth be told…everyone gave him a wide berth whenever possible.

One of our neighbours was Creusoise to her very core. Lucienne lived next door in a house that resembled a cavern. It was dark and slightly damp and she had a dog that wandered around the village piddling up every available pillar and post to mark out its territory.

She lived with her mother, a frail looking woman with no teeth who could smile at you or grimace at you and it was the same facial expression, so it was impossible to tell whether she was happy or in constant pain.

As lovely as Lucienne was, her roots were very much set down as a farmer's wife. Her husband had long since departed - divorced not dead - but to make ends meet she would do everything required to ensure she and her mother survived. She would be out in all weathers planting, tending and reaping her harvest of vegetables. She kept chickens for eggs and, afterwards, for eating, and kept her hedges at bay by spraying them with diesel; a slightly unusual method of border husbandry but very effective…as we found out when she forgot to turn the sprayer off on her tractor and it killed half our lawn.

One day, I went to check on our own chickens and found one of them very worse for wear. As much as I knew the right thing to do was to finish it off via a sharp knife or by using a more 'manual' method, I just couldn't do it. Being brought up in Ilford, my experience of killing chickens was limited as you would expect so I decided to enlist the help of the assassin next door. I went round and knocked on the door and was greeted by her mother. This wizened, toothless husk of a woman shrieked at me that Lucienne had gone out and would return later on that evening.

I said I would pop in the following day and get some advice on the best - and the most humane - way to put the afflicted chicken out of its misery.

That night, I went back to the hen house to find the aforementioned chicken as stiff as a board; clearly it had succumbed to whatever illness it had contracted and the need for intervention of any sort had passed...thankfully. Once again, I let Lucienne's mother know and she said she would tell Lucienne on her return.

Later on, and the saga of the chicken had been forgotten. We were relaxing in front of the television when the kitchen door flew back on its hinges and we were confronted by Lucienne, in full camouflage gear, screaming *"quelqu'un"* which is the French equivalent of "anyone home??"

Having been half asleep when she burst in, I levitated about three feet off of the sofa and let out a bellowing fart as back up. Trudy, thankfully, maintained full control of her colon but yelped as the door flew open, which made Ben leap off of the sofa and crap on the floor…it was carnage.

"I'm here to kill the chicken" she said. "No need, you maniac!" I replied "the bloody chicken died about 3 hours ago!" There was a pause "well if you need anything else killed, I can do it while I'm here with THIS!" and with that produced an 18" Bowie knife from behind her back. "Christ alive!!" I exclaimed "Put - the knife - DOWN! You're only making it worse for yourself!!"

She carefully re-sheathed the blade and started to retreat towards the front door.

"Yes – thank you very much for coming…I'll be in touch" I said, and closed the front door behind her making sure that all five locking points, the Chubb lock and the chain were in place before going back to the kitchen where Trudy was wiping up the remnants of Ben's faecal tsunami. "That woman" she exclaimed, pointing her finger at the now thankfully departed neighbour, "is a f****ng nutter!!" "I know dear" I replied "but even worse, she's a nutter with an array of murderous weapons at her very fingertips".

Having managed to 'talk down' the assassin next door and survive the night time stealth attack, we felt we might need to ingratiate ourselves into the village. Christmas was coming and we had arranged to see Jim and Yvette on Christmas day to take part in yuletide festivities and participate in some age-old Christmas day games such as the annual Brussel sprout and root vegetable eating competition – I felt particularly confident this year after coming so close to breaking the existing French all comers record last year of 36 sprouts and, having been in training for most of the winter by eating vegetable stew, I felt I could handle another half dozen at least.

This, along with blindfolding every one of the guests in turn, spinning them round and then see how long it took them to stuff an onion up the turkey's arse was what a traditional Christmas was all about…such fun!

In order for this to take place however, we needed a turkey. Luckily, we had a solution that would A) make the day of festivities a reality, and B) help ingratiate us into the village.

We spoke to one of our neighbours – Peg leg. To this day I don't know his real name; we just called him Peg leg. He was the unofficial boyfriend of the murderous neighbour next door and a farmer who at some point in his life had fallen into a piece of treacherous farming equipment and lost a leg. I did ask him once why he hadn't gone to the hospital and had it sewn back on to which he replied "because my leg was on one side of the machine and I was the other, and I couldn't stand up" Fair point if you think about it. I'll be honest, his one remaining leg was beautiful; in the words of Peter Cook and Dudley Moore 'I had nothing against his right leg...unfortunately neither did he'

I asked Peg leg if he could provide us with a turkey for Christmas. "Quelle Poids?" – what weight. "Sept kilos" I replied. Peg Leg gave me the thumbs up and said he would deliver it on Christmas Eve.

Sure enough, on Christmas Eve, Peg Leg arrived at the duly appointed time with a large box...a VERY large box. He limped his way into the kitchen looking like a hybrid between a gnarly old farmer and an NCP car park attendant. He proudly opened the box to reveal possibly the biggest turkey I had ever seen. It transpired that when I said seven kilos, he thought it was for seven *people* and as I hadn't specified a weight, he would give me what *HE* felt was the correct size...along with the commensurate price tag. Trudy was already contemplating stuffing it with the oven to get it cooked. "How much costa?" I asked, nervously, having seen the corpse that lay, prone, on my kitchen table. "Seventy euros" he said. "Sorry! For a minute there I misheard you and thought you said seventy euros!!" I laughed nervously. "Yes, that's right" he said, "...any chance of a drink? It IS Christmas" I recovered my composure and asked him if he wanted a beer or a pastice. He turned his nose up at both as if I had insulted the size of his manhood, but his eyes lit up when he saw that I had a bottle of whiskey on the shelf. Slightly begrudgingly I poured him a whiskey, which he gulped down and then showed me his empty glass which I took as meaning a refill was required. I duly obliged, as I did a third time at which point, thankfully, he said it was time to leave as he had other deliveries to do. I felt as though I had been mugged then ordered by the judge to be grateful for it.

Peg leg made his way – slightly less foot sure on his one remaining foot than previously – to the front door and I opened it for him. As he was confronted by the cold night air, he turned and looked at me with a cherubic smile on his face, took one step outside and then, very slowly, listed forward until he fell, face first, into the flower bed. Because he only had one leg, gaining enough purchase with his remaining leg on the gravel proved rather difficult and he went round in a big circle like he was break dancing. "Oh Christ!" said Trudy "quick! help him up!". "I can't" I replied, "This is hilarious! I'm pissing myself!!" With that, Peg leg managed to gain a foot hold against the stone border and hopped with his one good leg upwards and towards himself until he stood upright. "I...am...fine" he proclaimed - in English – much to the surprise of everyone gathered. He then jumped into his car and headed off up the road to his next delivery, weaving from side to side as he went.

Trudy looked at me. I looked at Trudy, "just go in and close the door love" I said. We did, and there was a reassuring click as the deadbolt engaged.

The following morning, having partaken of a cold compress to ease the shock of paying about £55.00 for a turkey, I decided to take Ben for a walk along the road and up to the next village, COUDERT. It had snowed heavily and the ground was covered by about six inches of pristine, virgin snow.

As we re-entered the village after our short walk - as mentioned previously, Ben was never one for unnecessary exercise - I saw a car, a Renault 4, recognisable as that belonging to Lucienne, the maniacal neighbour, parked outside the Maire's house. As I got closer, Lucienne appeared with Guy Jallot in tow; she was crying.

Having experienced her murderous demeanour when she *wasn't* in an emotional state of flux, I'll be honest, I was concerned. There was no telling what array of hand weapons she might decide to use and bearing in mind she was close to, and sometimes slightly over, the edge of sanity, this was worrisome indeed. I approached with my hand outstretched, "easy girl" I said in my calmest voice "easy now…friend". I then made a HUGE error. "…what's wrong?" I asked. I immediately knew I had made a schoolboy error and this was confirmed straight away by Guy standing behind her and waiving to me to make my escape while he distracted her. But it was too late; Lucienne looked at me, her eyes cold and dark like a prowling great white shark and she made a bee-line towards me like…well, a great white shark.

"What's wrong?" she said "I'll tell you what's wrong…come with me!" it wasn't so much an offer more like an ultimatum. With that she opened the car doors and directed myself, Guy and Ben into the car. Guy and I were slightly reticent to get in as we had seen her drive before.

Ben, on the other hand, leapt in with unbridled zeal and abandon as he followed the scent of various animals that had been shoved in the car and met their particularly sticky end as she slit them from neck to nuts on the back seat.

No sooner had the doors shut than she floored the accelerator and we hurtled through the village, fishtailing from side to side on the shingle road. No more than about a minute later, we arrived at her 'storage' facility (for 'storage' read abattoir) in the adjoining village, Petit Villard. We extricated ourselves from the blood wagon, Ben somewhat reluctantly, and she walked towards a small outbuilding, reminiscent of an old outside privy. As she reached it, she started digging with her hands and got down to about eight or nine inches before she brushed the snow aside to reveal half a frozen fish.

"Who would do this??" she asked. Guy shrugged his shoulders. "WHY would they do this??" "What does this mean??" "Perhaps their fridge broke" I said in a vain attempt to lighten the mood. Guy looked me askance, his eyes wide like dinner plates and I could see by the look on his face, this was no time for frivolous, impertinent comments. Lucienne then dug down again, slightly to one side of her initial excavation, where she exposed the tail end of the same fish.

"OH! THIS IS TOO MUCH!!" she said "Maire Jallot, I demand you make enquiries as to who would do such a thing!!" Guy agreed to use all of the resources available to him (that would be a none) to investigate the heinous act.

With that, her mood and demeanour lightened and she offered us a lift back. I declined on mine and Ben's behalf, leaving Guy as the sole passenger/victim for the return journey. He had no option, he was the Maire, he was obliged to...It came with the civic regalia. Ben whimpered as I dragged him out of the blood-wagon like he was saying goodbye to a long-lost friend and we waved as we watched the car being thrown along the village lane and disappear in an avalanche of snow and slush into the distance.

Chapter 11- Terror on the Tracks

The Creuse region of France is not known as a primary tourist destination. Farming? yes...tourists? not really. That said, it's a bit of a hidden gem. Lush green countryside, clear cool rivers...and cows...lots of cows.

There are approximately four times as many cows in Creuse as there are people – fact. With that being the case, the regional tourist board have, if truth be known, been 'nickin' a living' for the past few years and approached tourism and its promotion with a style and effort that can best be described as languid.

It came as a bit of a shock therefore, when we found out that there was a new tourist attraction in a town near us – Bourganeuf. The attraction itself was a 'Velo rail'. Bourganeuf itself has a large Turkish community and heritage, with tales of the Black Prince being held captive for ransom during the 15th Century in the tower situated in the middle of the town. He was there for some time apparently as Turkey decided he wasn't worth much and decided not to pay.

The small towns on its outskirts have a history of mining and you can still see the old mining rail tracks in and around some of its environs. One of these towns, Bosmoreau les Mines, was where the Velo rail was situated.

The commune had refurbished the mines rail line and had come up with the idea of using the route as a tourist trail. Visitors could sit on a 4-person rail cart, which had seats back and front, with the front wheels attached to, essentially, bicycle chains and pedals.

One could then pedal along the rail track and see the wonders of the Creuse whilst getting some gentle exercise. Well, that was the idea in theory; in practice it was somewhat different.

The track itself was a single-gauge track; absolutely fine until you met someone coming the other way, when a stand-off ensued to see who had right of way. The loser of the stand-off therefore, had to pick up their cart and place it on the grass verge until the oncoming traffic had passed, at which point you could then re-position the cart back on the tracks and continue.

The second 'fly' in this particular pot of ointment was that the carts weighed about 500 kgs so manhandling them was no easy feat. The third sticking point was that when you got to the other end, you had to pick the cart up, turn it round and pedal back. Call me old fashioned but it seemed a lot of lifting and hard work just to see some bison (there was and still is a bison park on the outskirts of Bourganeuf) and some piles of rubble, loosely resembling houses, and pay 20.00 euros a piece for the privilege!

Notwithstanding all of the above, Trudy and I, along with trusty sidekicks Jim and Yvette, decided to try out the new attraction in order that, should anyone who stayed in the chambre d'hotes ask us, we could report first hand on its efficiency and level of excitement on the 'Thrillometer'. We reserved our slot – as recommended by the operative in the tourist office – and turned up at the allotted time on what turned out to be one of the hottest days of the year.

We were given the normal, cursory lesson on how to sit down and use bike pedals, and then, without further ado, we set off. One of the attraction workers, complete with Hi-Viz jacket and red flag, was placed on crowd control duties and waved his flag furiously at the thronging crowd to alert them to our impending, high speed arrival. The thronging crowd was singularly disinterested, and he walked off to get an ice cream.

Jim and I were front and centre; this was no job for girlies. Jim's unnaturally long, deer-like calves glistened in the sun, as did my more normal manly shaped calves as we peddled furiously to get the chariot moving forward at an acceptable speed...synchronisation was key...Ben Hur it wasn't. The chairs on the chariot were basically plastic stacking chairs of the sort found in a school hall on parents evening that had been screwed to the floor of the chariot and, as we peddled, Trudy and Yvette chatted on the back two seats, oblivious to our efforts and exertions.

After about a quarter of a mile (we established that the round trip was about 3 miles) Trudy and Yvette demanded that they be given an opportunity to prove their abilities, so we swapped places. They seemed to be going faster than we were…Jim and I agreed that this was obviously as we had been going uphill…and we both relaxed in the back seats and started taking in the surrounding vista whilst chatting about nothing in particular.

It should be pointed out at this stage that we noticed that Trudy had quite a unique cycling style. The difference in height between 5'4" Trudy and 5'9" Yvette seemed to be predominately based on leg length and this meant that while Yvette was peddling at a cruising speed, Trudy was racing to keep up with the rotation speed of the pedals and that large circular thing with the teeth on it…the flywheel as it's known in the bike game – the effort of doing so making her sway from side to side.

Jim and I were still chatting when we looked round to the front to see that Trudy was nowhere to be seen; she'd gone. Disappeared. I looked at Jim, Jim looked at me and for some reason we looked under the seat...or where the seat should have been. The three remaining members of our group – me and the two serving police officers – looked at each other and then, as one, we looked behind us and there, lying on the ground in a ditch by the side of the rail track was Trudy; still sitting in her seat and trying to get up as though nothing had happened and there was nothing to see.

"What are you doing love?" I asked, knowing the instant I asked the question it was a stupid one, even by my standards.

"I don't know what happened!" she said. "...one minute I was peddling for all I was worth, next minute I was arse upwards in the ditch!"

Jim used all of his investigative skills, honed after 20 years' service in H.M Police service and presented his conclusion. "You broke it" he said, his renowned skill at stating the bleedin' obvious coming to the fore.

"...good job you're here Sherlock" we all replied in unison.

It transpired on further forensic examination that Trudy's relentless swaying and highly irregular style of peddling, combined with the clearly questionable manufacture and structural integrity of the bracket holding the seat onto the chariot, meant that the screws had been pulled clean out of the chariot deck, thus resulting in Trudy AND the chair exiting stage right into the ditch. Trudy, with a cut leg and damaged pride couldn't really throw any light on what had happened, suffice to say one minute she was peddling, the next she saw the ground rushing up to meet her.

After checking she was unhurt, and making sure we got a photo for social media purposes - obviously - we then had to make a decision on whether to continue or not. The decision was a relatively easy one to make as the chariot now only had one serviceable seat at the front and, therefore, only one set of working peddles. It had been hard enough to pedal with two people but with only one person taking up the strain it was nigh on impossible. It would have taken someone with the staying power of a triathlete and thighs of teak to move it so we decided to turn back.

As previously mentioned, turning the chariot around involved physically picking up the chariot and placing it back on the tracks. This was a lot easier said than done and took some time. Having used the British rail network for over 35 years, and having experienced the delays due to someone having a twisted sock at Highbury Corner, I can only assume that this is exactly the same method incorporated by most of the rail franchises, although I would also add that the 25 minutes it took us to efficiently execute a full 180 degree turn was a significantly shorter delay than Network Rail and the perennially delayed service from Kings Cross to Peterborough, as those unfortunate enough to endure the service on a daily basis, I have no doubt, will bear testament to.

Having managed to pick up the chariot and synchronise our movements so that we were all trying to move in the same, circular direction - you wouldn't believe how tricky this could be when one of you is left-handed and the three others refused to agree on which way was counter clockwise - we decided that we would take turns in sitting in the one remaining seat and use the one remaining set of functioning pedals whilst the others pushed the terminally lame chariot for all they were worth.

As mentioned previously, it was one of the hottest days of the year... the return trip was also uphill. With Trudy taking up position on the seat and using her unique style of pedalling, and with Jim on one side of the chariot, me on the other side and Yvette bringing up the rear, we set off to get the stricken handcar back to the depot.

What with the searing heat – it was north of 90 degrees – and with me having taken the decision prior to setting off to take the opportunity to wear my newly purchased wide brimmed safari hat to protect my balding pate, eye-witness accounts at the time suggested that they had witnessed an updated version of the popular 80s drama series Tenko. As much as this was, regrettably, wrong, you can see how the mistake could be made with two women struggling to move a half-ton rail carriage up an incline whilst two blokes – one in a large khaki hat – 'encouraged' them from afar.

Having reached the sanctity of the depot, we reported the incident to the man in charge who looked at the gap where the second chair should have been, pointed and asked "ou est le siège?" *where is the seat?*

We took the opportunity to retrieve the somewhat buckled chair from behind the back seat and dropped it at his feet. "you've broken it!" he said "...not so much broken it as redesigned it" we replied "however you will notice my good man that it has, in return, redesigned my wife's shins". He took a look at Trudy's shins which were oozing blood "she looks like she's rolled down an embankment" he said, chuckling. "Funny you should say that laughing boy" said Trudy, as she walked towards him with her fists clenched, cracking her knuckles.

Fortunately for him, he picked up on her humourless demeanour quite quickly. "Ah, yes! yes! I see, please avail yourselves of a free refreshment and it would pleasure me to give you twenty euros reduction on your next visit". "I'll have the twenty euros" I said "but there's no need to pleasure yourself on our behalf...bit rude to be honest"

Since that day we have visited Bourganeuf countless times and indeed have seen other poor unsuspecting souls setting off on a seemingly innocent trip on the velorail. As they leave, we see them smiling in anticipation; how many *actually* make it back? I couldn't possibly say.

What I do know is that sometimes, I'm told, when the wind blows in the right direction and the moonlight shines down on the rail tracks in *just* the right way, you can hear the 'clickety clack', 'clickety clack' of train wheels on the tracks, the 'thwack' of a bamboo stick-on buttock and the faint murmur of Japanese as lost souls return wearily to the engine shed.

Chapter 12 – Le Doux Amer Restaurant

Our nearest town was a little town called Ahun (…pronounced 'a-arn'…) It was some 6kms away from Villard but had all of the essentials we needed; boulangerie (x2), bar, supermarket, vet, bar, doctor, dentist, oh…and a bar. Basically, everything a normal person would need on an everyday basis.

One of the more diverse services on offer in Ahun was a restaurant called the Doux Amer. On the face it, the Doux Amer seemed like a perfectly normal restaurant. Open at lunchtimes only, it provided a 3-course meal at a very reasonable price (about 15 euros a person) and was extremely popular with tradesmen and workers in the locality. The restaurant itself had been started and was run as part of a community project, and the one feature of the establishment that was slightly out of the ordinary, was that some of the people who worked there had learning difficulties and working at the restaurant was part of the process of helping them integrate into the local community. It was a good cause and, happily, was well supported by the local community.

Having always meant to sample its delights and having been recommended to do so, we decided one Christmas to book a table for us, Jim and Yvette and two other friends. We arrived at the duly appointed time and were met at the entrance to the establishment by a smiling 'proprietaire'. We told him we had a reservation and, without any further ado, we were shown to our table.

As we arrived at the table, simultaneously a young girl appeared. Having not even had the chance to sit down or indeed bend a knee as a pre-cursor to sitting down, she thrust a tray towards us which held six glasses of a blue liquid. Unsure of the contents, I gave it what's known as the 'thousand-yard stare'. We all took the glasses like the trained lab rats we were and I wished her a hearty 'Merry Christmas' at which point she looked me squarely in the face, turned a full 180 degrees and ran away back to the kitchen. I'd like to say this was an unusual reaction but to be honest, my success with women during my legendary and oft discussed adolescent 'permed hair' period of the mid to late 1970s, would suggest otherwise. Nothing that I knew of was that colour, other than paint or Nitromors and, as far as I was aware, necking Farrow and Ball Parma Ham was NOT a Christmas tradition I was particularly keen to adopt. I looked at Jim, Jim looked at me and, as one, we all emptied the contents of our glasses into the conveniently positioned potted plant that was at the side of our table which, it has to be said, was looking very well-watered. This suggested to us that perhaps it was well accustomed to being the recipient of whatever the hell the blue liquid was and this made us feel slightly better…I suggest significantly better than the drink would have made us feel.

No sooner had we sat down than our waitress appeared again, tray aloft, with our starters. I'm not sure what it was but the colour suggested either very young cheese or very old meat. Having discarded the aperitifs, it seemed churlish to do it again so straws were drawn to see who would take first bite; the plan being, if they survived, the rest of us would dive in. Suffice to say, after a brief delay, we all tucked in.

To all of our surprise, no-one died, and, once we had all finished, and after a little coaxing from the side-lines, our young waitress appeared again to clear away the empty plates. As we sat there chatting and generally soaking up the festive atmosphere, we marvelled at the effort that had been made in putting up the Christmas decorations and the large Christmas tree, burgeoning with sparkling garlands, balls and lights. It was a feast and a treat for the eyes.

No sooner had we marvelled at the beautiful surroundings and ambiance, than one of the waiters came charging out of the kitchen, nearly taking the saloon style swing doors off their hinges in the process and, at full tilt, ran straight into the Christmas tree which toppled over, shedding its glittering adornments over half the restaurant. He then attempted to catch the tree and put it back up but, sadly, ended up straddling the trunk and riding it across the room like Seabiscuit. It was terminal as only the top 18" remained intact and, after realising it was doomed, he dropped it to the floor and gave the top of the tree to one his colleagues, who stood there holding it like a 5-year-old holding a sparkler, looking around the room for guidance as to what to do next. After a minute or so he turned full circle, threw the morsel of tree to the floor like he'd been electrocuted and made his escape back to the kitchen.

With all this going on at once, we missed the return of our young waitress who had started to empty the contents of her tray onto our table. The contents appeared once again to resemble either very young cheese or very old meat and you could be forgiven in thinking that we had received a second round of starters.

We looked at it and it didn't take long before we all came to the conclusion that we had, indeed, been given a second round of starters. We looked at each other, shrugged and ate them. Unsurprisingly it tasted EXACTLY the same as it did 10 minutes previously, but it was ok then and it was ok now...no harm, no foul.

The intrigue and tension mounted exponentially as we all sat and waited for our main course. Would it actually be a main course, would it be a **THIRD** round of starters…who knew for sure.

The suspense was palpable as we caught sight of the waitress, shuffling towards us with a tray fully laden with food. Slightly disappointingly she proceeded to serve plates of main courses…I say serve…It would have been easier had we shouted "PULL!" in turn, and she threw them at us like a clay pigeon shoot. Having had the foresight to cover my front with a head-to-toe napkin, this caused no ill-effect and, whilst it was, technically, a tray of main courses, we couldn't actually be 100% certain they were *our* main courses, but we took them anyway and started eating them before anyone asked for them back. There was food being launched from all angles, I'm sure it was raining consommé soup at one point but eventually the gravy tsunami subsided and we settled down into our places. We cast an eye around the restaurant as tables of people chatted with each other, discussing what they had been served and how close it actually was to what they had ordered…invariably not very if truth be told.

There were people walking across the restaurant delivering plates of food to other tables and trying to work out if there was an algorithm involved or a probability ratio that calculated if table A had the food originally ordered by table C, and they were table H,

which table, in all probability, would be most likely to have THEIR food. It was like having front row seats to the shittiest game show ever. In the end, we all decided, after taking a quick 'round the room' straw poll, to just eat whatever was in front of you and have done with it! The motion was carried and seconded by the local doctor.

It truly was the most wonderful time of the year.

Chapter 13 – A Life On The Ocean Waves

In an attempt to give ourselves some free time from running the chambre d'hotes, we decided to buy ourselves a small pleasure boat. *'L'Aïgo'* we were told was an African word meaning 'sea' although I remain unconvinced as the only translation I can find says it's a kind of French provincial soup or a Korean term meaning 'Oh God!'. As you are about to find out, I tend to lean towards the latter. Being aware of the naval tradition of bringing bad luck upon us by changing the name, and despite having a boat called either 'Herbal soup' or 'Oh God' we kept it and pleaded ignorance to all who questioned the name. It was small - and I mean small - about 7 feet from bow to stern, open top with two bench seats and a 10hp engine. It was, however, perfect for what we wanted which was to potter around the nearby lake with Ben and Holly our canine companions whilst looking for places inaccessible to the great general public where we could stop and have tiffin…or a barbecue. It was also very portable – one person could pretty much pick it up - and the whole thing was a hybrid 'mash up' of Grace Kelly and 'Driving Miss Daisy' with me in the role of chauffeur/driver/captain, and Ben taking the lead role of Miss Daisy; a role in which he excelled.

We bought *L'Aïgo* from a young chap who lived near Carcassone. He used it for sea fishing and lived with his blonde, bronzed, statuesque girlfriend in a Mediterranean style house with a balcony which was covered with purple bougainvilleas. He looked like pretty much the coolest dude I'd ever seen as he laid back on his hammock in his cut down denim shorts, chewing on one of the pieces of straw from his hat. He was far too good looking for my liking and had one of those faces that needed punching to 'ugly him up' a bit and give the rest of us a fighting chance. I both hated him and loved him at the same time. We did the deal, paid the necessary 'reddies' and set back off on the trip home. I would have to say we must have cut quite a dash as we headed up the motorway with our pocket-sized boat behind us, based on the amount of people who were pointing at us and laughing. When we got home, we quickly popped the boat in the barn, covered it with a face flannel and looked forward to our first nautical trip.

We had many great days out, accompanied by Jim and Yvette in their boat which normally involved me getting wet, Trudy shouting at me and telling me what an unrelenting arsehole I was, and the boat breaking down in one way or another. To put some flesh on the bone of this, there are two incidents that stand out.

On one such occasion, the weather seemed set fair and we decided to go out for the day with our trusty sidekicks and have a picnic at the lake. We knew a small spot that was rarely used during the week and we had no-one booked into the chambre d'hotes so off we went.

We arrived, transferred the picnic goods, along with some fold-up chairs into Jim and Yvette's boat, a new, smaller, RIB type boat which they had procured after trading in the St Tropez version (see chapter 4 if you're interested) - no chance of getting anything in ours as anything heavier than a crusty baguette could upset the ballast and would, in all likelihood, capsize us - and off we set.

Half way across the lake there was an audible 'TWANG' and I lost all power and drive.

The steering and power mechanism used on an outboard motor is either via the 'tiller', a long arm-like structure that extends from the engine casing, moves the engine left and right and also has a fitting on the end that provides power when you twist it, or via a couple of cables that lead from the engine itself, down one side to a box where one of the cables is attached to a throttle lever, for forward and backward momentum, and the other extends further to a steering wheel which, when turned, turns the rudder and, hey presto, the boat steers.

Having only a very limited set of tools with me...let me put that another way...having NO tools with me,

I was somewhat stymied as to what to do next. No amount of pushing and pulling on the throttle lever made the boat move forward and we floated aimlessly on the lake unable to move.

Jim and Yvette did what all good friends would do and left us to start the picnic; after all, they were hungry and had all of the food. I stared at the throttle lever housing as if looking at it would somehow repair it by ESP, and then, more by luck than judgement, realised that we did still have *backward* motion. It was better than nothing…but only just.

Trudy helped by telling me that I was not ONLY an arsehole but a "useless tosspot" t'boot, which obviously made me feel significantly better… good job I know she loves me with an undying passion or it would hurt my feelings.

Gently, I eased the boat into reverse and we started to move, albeit slowly, across the water. Growing in confidence I 'opened her up' and, with water cascading over the stern which wasn't designed to be the front-end, and nearly drowning the dogs who were sitting in the back, we made our way across the lake to meet up with our Jim and Yvette.

The sight of us coming around the corner, backwards, was almost too much for them to bear and Jim almost choked on his 'pate de fois gras' as we moored up, back end in first on the bank.

"Glad you could make it" he said.

"Piss off you lanky twat" I said, as I searched frantically for something resembling food that was left from the picnic to take my mind off the morning's calamitous escapade.

Trudy said nothing, but looked at Yvette, closed her eyes and slowly shook her head. It was all SO familiar that it didn't even surprise her any more.

Later on, at about a quarter past port and lemon, we decided to go across the lake to the café that was situated on the shores of the lake. It was very picturesque; the sun was shining and we all felt it was time for a delicious ice cream. Clearly, our boat wasn't seaworthy - unless going backwards was deemed acceptable. We decided, therefore, to all go in Jim and Yvette's boat. Technically speaking it could seat about 6 people but with all the picnic luggage it was a bit of a squeeze. Factor in our two dogs, Ben (Miss Daisy) and Holly (the pocket rocket) as well as their two dogs, two black Labradors, Maggsy and Pip and the boat was stuffed to its rafters. This didn't deter Jim from heading off across the lake at full tilt, his excuse being "…it will be smoother once we're up on the plane…" for the uninitiated, the 'plane' is where the speed of the boat lifts it up and on top of the water, thereby using less fuel and, in effect, making the boat 'skip' across the top; a bit like when a stone skips across the top of a pond.

Whilst this was technically correct, the fact that the engine wasn't powerful enough to get the boat, the luggage, four adults and four dogs up on the plane meant that all we succeeded in doing was hit the waves and the wake of other boats at high speed. One of these boats was the official sight-seeing boat that cruises around the lake and on which party goers and gentry can have dinner and a few glasses of cold refreshment. This boat is about 100 feet long, about 40 feet wide and weighs about 15 tonnes. It will not take a genius to work out that the engine to push this around the lake was sizeable and, ergo, the wake it produces is substantial. Jim followed the time-honoured tradition of always crossing paths with another vessel to its rear and with a shout of *'BRACE YOURSELVES!!'* to the rest of us, we careered into its wake. The front of the boat went up into the air about 4 feet and crashed down onto the water showering the occupants with the contents of the picnic hamper and distributing the dogs liberally across its floor. The sound of claws raking at the floor of the boat could be heard as they four dogs tried in vain to get some purchase on the metal sheeting that made up the base of the boat. No sooner had we managed to get a semblance of order over proceedings than we saw Ben slowly rising up off of the floor. As he did so, he looked at me as if to say "…what exactly is going on you human halfwit??" At first, I had no idea myself but then it became apparent that when we had hit the wake of the cruising boat, everything had gone up in the air and landed on top of each other; picnic, chairs, bags, dogs, humans…and life vests.

As he landed, Ben had landed and sat on one of the life vests that Jim insisted on having on the boat…mainly because he was nothing if not thorough. Hitting the wake had also liberally doused the entire boat in quite an amount of water, and this water had set off the automatic inflation device that was in the life vest. We watched as Ben's rear end slowly lifted up into the air until he was balanced only on his two front legs in what looked remarkably like Yashtanga Yoga. Yoga it might have been, but his chakras were definitely not aligned as every attempt to get him down off of his impromptu perch was met with a snarl and I was forced to compensate him for his ignominious situation by offering him a half-eaten sausage roll, a remnant from the picnic, as reparations.

Slowly, we got him down off of his throne and he gave us his usual *'what has my life become? I don't have to put up with this'* face.

The life vest was now useless. Once the auto – inflation device has gone off it has to be replaced which it was.

Ben never set foot on their boat again without signing a disclaimer drawn up by his agent.

At the end of the season, a season marred only by 'the great Ben incident of 2008' and the 'backwards only' debacle, we had to winterise the boat. This is not a difficult task but you have to ensure that every drop of water is drained from the engine, or you risk destroying the engine if it freezes.

Winters in Creuse can be harsh. Temperatures of -15 are not uncommon; the first winter we arrived, it reached -20 and -26 on higher ground...as my old dad used to say 'taters'...don't ask me, I've got no idea what it means.

The condition of the boat engine and the effectiveness of the winterisation at those temperatures is very much in the lap of the Gods and, alas, our engine fell afoul of the weather. The following spring when we tried to start it for the first time it was clear that the main body of the engine had frozen and cracked and we had no option but to buy a new engine. A few weeks and quite a few euros later and we were back on the water, again with Jim and Yvette in tow.

We had repaired the 'no forward motion only backwards' issue which turned out to be the cable which had slipped out of its connection in the throttle lever housing and was easily fixed. With new engine all fired up and ready to go, we headed off to the lake.

The lake in question, Lac de Vassiviere, is one of the largest man-made lakes in Europe. Owned by EDF it is also used as a source of hydro-electric power as they drain the lake each year and feed the water into the neighbouring rivers. It covers 2500 acres, is 105 feet deep and is approximately 30 kms in circumference. It is popular without being over popular and visitors can enjoy its facilities and walks, sometimes, without seeing another soul. Even the summer holiday period is not overly packed, save a few boats and a few ramblers.

Our trip out at the start of the season meant we were pretty much the only ones on the lake and we shared it with some fishermen who watched as we launched the boats successfully off the slipway and meandered our way across the water, following our noses, no particular route, just enjoying the warm spring sunshine.

The fishermen were still there when we returned a few hours later and, again, they watched as we moored up on the jetty and reversed the cars down the slipway ready to retrieve the boats out of the water.

I was first with Jim still moored up at the jetty.

Getting a boat out of the water can be significantly more difficult than getting it into the water. This is because the water moves with any wind or breeze that might be around and this affects the way the boat handles in the water. It's also more difficult if the boat in question is in the hands of an imbecile.

Boat engines are made so that they CANNOT start if they are in gear. The throttle lever MUST be in the 'idle' position and in 'neutral'. It is impossible to start a boat in gear.

The ignition on my boat was via a key, and had a 'deadman's cord' which is designed to be wrapped around the driver's arm or leg and clipped onto the ignition. This is supposed to cut the engine should the driver fall overboard. It is an imperative piece of kit and every conscientious boat owner wears one when on the water. I was no different and was wearing my cord as I turned the key but there was no response. The engine wouldn't turn, I was dead in the water.

The one mistake I had made was that I had untied myself from the jetty so was floating in the open water.

Fortunately, the boat also had a pull cord arrangement for this very scenario, which allowed me to pull the cord and start the engine; much like a lawn mower. I carefully got onto the back seat of the boat and positioned myself to be able to pull the cord.

With a sharp tug the engine fired up.

At this point, I would like to take you back to my previous statement of how it is IMPOSSIBLE to start a boat when it is in gear. I quickly found out that it was not impossible but, in fact, quite the opposite.

The boat was in gear and the throttle lever pushed firmly forward when the engine kicked into life, the boat leaping forward like a scalded cat. The sudden, violent movement threw me onto the back seat. I managed to land on the back seat and throw myself forward all in one movement.

I landed in the footwell at the front of the boat and yanked the steering wheel 'hard 'a' port' as the boat careered towards the wall of the slipway…and the three fisherman who had been watching the farce unfold. As the boat lurched hard left, they calmly lifted up their rods and the attached lines one by one as I passed within a hair's breadth of the stone wall they were sitting on.

Still sitting in the footwell, I looked back at Jim.

Never have I seen a man adopt the purply reddish hue he had and still be alive. He was laughing to such an extent he couldn't breathe. All I could see was his pearly white teeth against his red face and neck. He looked like a 'No Entry' sign.

A full 15 minutes later and he still couldn't compose himself enough to attempt to get his boat out of the water.

Trudy, who had been watching from the safety of the car said nothing but, as before, looked at Yvette, closed her eyes and slowly shook her head. Once again, it was all SO familiar that it didn't even surprise her any more.

To this day, Jim swears it is the funniest thing he has ever seen or witnessed, but, remarkably, is almost gushing in his admiration for the way I managed to avoid the wall AND the fishermen… all whilst sitting arse upwards in the footwell of the boat…high praise indeed.

Chapter 14 – The Legend of 'Daktari' Doug

While all of this was going on, there was a diminutive man somewhere in Staffordshire, going about his daily business.

Doug Bennett, a diminutive figure of 5'5" was an ex-Royal Marine Commando who fought in the Burma Campaign and was the step-father of Yvette (Jim's wife) along with her sister and brother. Yvette always called him 'pop' and, in the end, I think he was 'pop' to us all. Doug was one of those characters who were funny without even trying, and never used one word where a hundred would do the job just as well. He became a bit of a legend in our eyes and this due, in no small part, to the fact that he was a huge fan and exponent of the beige, three-quarter length trouser. Some men can carry this off - David Beckham carries this off whilst also wearing one of Posh's frocks – but Doug was neither an ex-Manchester United and England footballer, nor was he a fashion icon. However, undeterred and dressed in his holiday safari suit, he became known affectionately as 'Daktari Doug'. Doug was a true midlands man; when he spoke, you couldn't help but laugh at him and love him at the same time. He had a turn of phrase that was hilarious and completely unprepared…which was what made it hilarious.

He also had a voice that got higher and higher as he got more excited to the point whereby at his peak, it was only audible to dogs.

On an annual basis, Doug and his wife Gwen would set off from home and drive down to stay with Jim and Yvette for their summer holidays. Gwen didn't say an awful lot but what she did say was generally succinct and worth listening to. Doug made up for it and would talk to anyone and, despite the fact that he spoke not a single word of French, would always make himself understood.

As an example of this, they once checked in to a hotel on their trip back to the UK without a reservation and, when confronted by the Concierge, Doug uttered not a word. He simply pointed to himself, pointed to Gwen, placed the palms of his hands together as if praying then placed them under his head on the reception counter as if asleep, at which point he did fake snoring then looked at the Concierge for confirmation. They got a room immediately. At the end of the day, I suppose it matters not one jot HOW you get a room as long as you do and his method worked perfectly. One assumes the task was made no easier for him by the fact that in all likelihood he could barely see over the reception desk!

Everyone looked forward to seeing Doug and Gwen and we always went out with them for a couple of trips when they were in France.

One year, we were informed that there was big news…Doug had bought a new car. The big day arrived and Doug and Gwen arrived in their new mode of transport – a Citroen C5 saloon with all mod cons.

When they arrived, the first task was to give anyone who was interested (…and some that weren't if truth be known) a full, in-depth tour of the vehicle and a full demonstration of the various extras and accoutrements that came with the car.

These included but were not restricted to:

- Heated seats
- Fold back wing mirrors
- Electric seat adjustment

We arrived and got the full manufacturers demonstration as did other people who arrived, each of us 'cooed' in the right places and Doug was very happy. One of our friends was given the demo and to emphasise the luxurious nature of the vehicle, Doug sat in the driver's seat and operated the electric adjustment facility of the front seats.

"Watch this Sandra" said Doug.

Sandra waited with baited breath and watched eagerly as Doug pressed the button. There was almost imperceivable movement as Doug gradually moved forward, millimetre by millimetre, closer to the steering wheel.

"That's incredible Doug" said Sandra, ever the diplomat and not really knowing what it was that she was supposed to be admiring.

One of Doug's favourite trips was to Gueret, our biggest local town and capital of the Creuse. He loved visiting Carrefour, the biggest supermarket in the area, which had all manner of goods, a variety of small outlets on its concourse and a café. Doug would like nothing more than to sit and watch the locals going about their business, picking up fruit, putting down fruit, complain about the price, complain about the way the shop was laid out... basically complain.

His observations would be accompanied by side comments as he saw someone walk past.

"Look at him Jim! The bloke in the brown hat"

Jim would look round...

"That man has got the longest nose hairs I've ever seen on a bloke" "I bet every time he sneezes, he must lash himself to the nearest lamppost!"

He had a comment and an answer for almost everything. On one occasion when visiting the gentlemen's facilities, Jim who is broadly recognised as having a bladder the size of a salted peanut, went too and, when they went in, the cleaner – a lady – was cleaning the area. Jim, having experienced this previously, unashamedly unzipped his trousers and proceeded to go about his business. Doug was horrified. When they came out, he couldn't wait to relay what had happened to Gwen.

"There we are Gwen" his voice already reaching the equivalent of an F sharp "ready to have a slash, and I turned to Jim and I said to him Jim! There's a cowing woman in the toilets and you're there farting like a madman!!"

Having visited the same facilities a couple of trips later, Doug was gone for ages. In the end, so much time had elapsed that Yvette sent Jim to start a search and rescue mission. Jim came upon Doug washing his hands and enquired what had taken so long.

"I'll tell you what took so bleedin' long! No toilet seat! I'm not squatting on cold ceramic for anyone so I had to fashion a seat out of toilet paper! What sort of country doesn't have toilet seats!! Bleedin' barbarians the lot of 'em!!"

Doug and Gwen were very well travelled and went on some very nice holidays to some exotic locations. On one such holiday they went to Thailand on a cruise and, after a couple of days and when they had settled into their accommodation decided to spend the day on the beach. As mentioned previously, Doug was of diminutive stature. With that in mind, when one of the local girls came up to him and asked him if he would like a massage he jumped at the chance. His description of what followed went like this:

"Well our Yvette, this bird asked me if I wanted a massage so I thought well why not? She told me to lay face down on the sand which I did and she then proceeded to beat the livin' crap out of me!!" "By the time she'd finished pummelling me, she'd hit me so many times and so hard, I was level with the sand!!

He loved travelling but was very much a 'meat and two veg' kind of man. He once described pizza as 'a load of old muck on a load of old dough' and, whilst I admit, I am very partial to a pizza, his description was nothing if not accurate. He also had set views on certain things...one of which was conservatories and orangeries.

For years he flatly refused to have either until finally he cracked under pressure from Gwen.

Afterwards he couldn't have been happier, proclaiming that:

"…for years I hated the thought of a conservatory but I was wrong; basically, for years, I was a pratt…".

He also announced that they were therefore, now in the market for raffia furniture.

"…if you've got a conservatory Jim, protocol dictates you simply *must* have raffia furniture…"

His stories and adventures weren't confined to foreign climes. If something was going to happen, it would happen to Doug. When at home in Staffordshire, he happened one day upon a salesman who was selling mobility scooters. Doug had no need for a mobility scooter but his question "wha'tve you got there Jack?" - not the chap's name but anyone he didn't know was Jack - was a precursor to a 30 minute demonstration and sales pitch by the salesman, the result of which was that Doug bought the mobility scooter. Jim and Yvette tell a story of how they made him go out with them a few years later and, on reaching their destination and having loaded the mobility scooter into the back of their car, Doug confessed that he had left the keys at home. Not letting this stand in their way, they proceeded to push Doug up hill and down dale while he sat in the scooter, at one point watching, laughing, as they hit a downhill stretch and the scooter picked up speed over a cobbled street. All they saw was the scooter weaving from side to side and Doug fighting the controls as he bounced up and down until he nearly lost all of his fillings.

This was not his only purchase of comedic value. Jim and Yvette visited one day and he was sitting in his lounge on a new armchair. He demonstrated that when he pressed a button on the side, the chair gently leaned forward and raised him up until he was standing.

It had been procured and set up by the company that delivered it and when he got it, he was very happy. He demonstrated the workings to Jim and Yvette and, much like the Citroen C5, the movement was almost imperceivable. That said, eventually Doug was upright and in a standing position. He had also purchased a new doorbell. One of the types where you press the button and it rings in the kitchen using radio waves from the main box in the hall; all very impressive.

A few days later Yvette happened to phone him and asked how everything was with his new purchases. Needless to say it was not without incident.

Doug had been sitting on his new chair and the doorbell rang. He pressed the button on the chair and slowly...very slowly...the chair raised him up to a standing position. He went to the front door, opened it and found no-one there. He had a quick look round to see if anyone was loitering, there wasn't so he closed the front door and went back inside.

Not 10 minutes later it happened again. Doug pressed the button and in much the same way, the chair raised him up to his full height whereupon he went and opened the front door to be greeted by no-one. Slightly annoyed by the inconvenience, he shut the door a bit more vigorously than before and went back to his chair.

10 minutes later, and for a third time, the doorbell rang. Doug pressed the button on the chair like he had never pressed it before, stood up and walked with purpose up to the front door. He threw the door open, saw there was no-one there, marched half way up his front garden path, clenched his fist, raised it to the air and shouted: "…bleedin' kids!! I know who you are! I'll give you a bleedin' good hidin' if I catch you"

He then marched inside, slammed the door and went back in the lounge and sat down.

However, this wasn't the end of the tale. For it wasn't children at all. It appeared, after a few phone calls and further investigation, that when the doorbell had been set up during installation, the installer had set it to the same frequency as used by the buses on the route that passed outside Doug's front door. Therefore, every time someone wanted to get off the bus and rang the onboard bell, Doug's front doorbell rang!

Alas, neither Doug nor Gwen are with us any longer. Doug passed away in April 2017 but even at his funeral, he managed to give everyone a laugh.

On the day of the funeral, Doug was to be dressed by the undertakers in his best suit but the only one that could be found was a velvet dinner suit with very large lapels.

It was decided that this was not appropriate; as one of Yvette's relatives pointed out "...you can't bury him looking like Jimmy Tarbuck".

RIP Daktari Doug - 'Pops' to all who knew him.

Chapter 15 – The Clown Car

As our business became more successful, it also became apparent that we needed to invest a bit of money in equipment. We had most of what was required but we were taking everything around on a trailer which was being pulled by our car, A Renault Megane saloon that had belonged to our friends in the UK and which we had, up to that point, also been using as our normal run-around. With that in mind we decided to get something that we could use solely for gardening and generally hauling heavy stuff around. We decided that, due to the climatic conditions we sometimes had to endure, that a 4x4 was a minimum requirement and we settled on a Toyota Hilux SURF which was big, strong and fitted the bill.

We saw one advertised in the UK and, having agreed a price, bought it, subject to all things being OK. We then made a trip back to the UK to collect it.

On collecting the car, it was decided that I would drive the new car back and follow Trudy who knew the route by heart. Apart from almost missing the ferry due to a holdup on the M25, the journey went off without incident. Compared to the Renault Megane, it was a bit juicy and we had to refill a couple of times and, understandably it was a bit more sluggish than the Megane.

Having got back to France unscathed, I decided to take it out on its first, meaningful trip and so, with trailer attached and laden with gardening equipment, we set off.

I should point out at this stage that I know virtually nothing about cars or the detailed workings of the combustion engine. The workings of flange pins and the legendary gangle iron means nothing to me; and don't get me started on the giubo, the gudgeon pin or the Wankel rotary engine.

What I did know was that it seemed a bit sluggish...especially uphill. It was an automatic and on the side of the 'gear' lever was a red button with Japanese writing above it. I had no idea what it did and decided I was not the right person to try it and see what happened.

What I didn't know about engines, my friend Terry did. Ex-British services (Royal Engineers), he had two main skill-sets. One was the repair and renovation of old cars and the other was concrete plinths. I asked him once whether the plinth we had built would be strong enough for the customers' requirements to which he replied "I should bloody well hope so – the last one of these I built had a Harrier Jump jet on it". I took that as a yes and we moved on. Terry came round with a selection of tools and diagnosed the problem as a faulty turbo or turbo pipe which meant that the engine was trying to shift a two-tonne car plus trailer with what was effectively about as much power as would normally struggle to pull the skin from a rice pudding. To repair it would cost about as much as the car cost in the first place so we decided to leave it and just 'make do'.

This decision meant that the car went from 0-60 in about two and a half days and its lack of power and, in some instances, any form of forward motion, became 'quite the talking point'.

It had a list of unusual 'foibles' which included:

- The mysterious Japanese red button – the purpose of which no amount of research on the internet could determine
- An electric back window that decided on its own whether to go up or down…regardless of the weather or if the engine was actually on.
- A four-wheel drive 'lock' button that you could engage whilst driving along but which would only disengage by turning left
- Headlights that filled up with water
- A starter motor that would sometimes stick and which then had to be hit with a piece of wood to make it work and start the car.

- No heater (always nice when its -15 outside) and when combined with the window suddenly opening in the middle of winter, it sometimes snowed INSIDE the car.

On the upside it did keep meat and other fresh produce edible for an extra couple of days.

Hills, slopes or even a gentle gradient were the cars nemesis and any route had to be calculated to avoid any such obstacles. Should you find yourself approaching any of the above, the agreed protocol was to either:

A) Floor it and hope for the best
B) Stop and put the LOW drive gear in place which allowed you to get to the top of the incline but did mean you then had to stop at the top and put the car back into the normal DRIVE gear.

Option B did sometimes cause consternation if you had a lorry behind you and suddenly stopped dead to change gear…oh how they laughed when we did that. Faced with a decision one day after pulling out of a car park onto a 5% incline, I chose option B and was promptly overtaken by a jogger and had a 50cc Microcar race up behind me and put its hazard lights on to warn traffic that there was a car in distress!

The countryside around Creuse is nothing if not hilly and many of our customers lived in places where hills were unavoidable. One solution I discovered when on my way to one customer was to press the accelerator firmly to the floor on the approach to the hill then turn sharp right into the car park of a garden nursery, scream through the car park, turning right again onto the road and use the 'sling shot' effect of both turning right and the weight of the vehicle to propel me up the hill.

Undeterred, we decided one day to load up the car – which had been affectionately named the 'Clown Car' on the grounds that with its countless idiosyncrasies and penchant for suddenly malfunctioning in some way or another, every journey turned into a circus, and head off to our nearest skiing resort, Mont D'or, in our neighbouring department - Puy de Domes - with Jim and Yvette and two other friends all crammed in the car; plus of course the four dogs. In hindsight, the ratio of power to weight meant that even had the car been functioning at its peak and to its full capacity, it might have struggled but in its present condition, and with the pulling power of a day-old poodle, we were doomed from the start. The journey consisted of us trying to estimate and calculate when we should go for maximum power, then stopping to apply 'LOW' gear, then normal DRIVE, followed by revving the engine to within an inch of its life, barely making it to the crown of a hill then breaking the land speed record on the downhill sections of the route. In what seemed like two days but what was, in fact only about two hours and, having reached Mont D'or, we parked up to let the engine cool down, and the brake pads stop smouldering. We spent a very pleasant afternoon in the town, eating, drinking and generally enjoying ourselves until it was decided that it was time to grasp the nettle and start the journey home.

At the time, Mont D'or was undergoing somewhat of a renovation with the roads being repaired and everywhere having a bit of a clean-up. As we shoe-horned ourselves back into the car, it very quickly became apparent that we were in a whole heap of trouble.

The road out of the town itself was being repaired and there was a diversion in place which directed traffic around the town centre, re-joining the main road a mile or so further on. The diversion included some temporary traffic lights which were set half way up a road with a shallow incline, turning into a 30-degree incline after 100 or so metres. I looked at Jim, Jim looked at me, we all looked at each other and uttered the same words "…We've got no chance…" "Have faith!!" I cried and as the lights turned green, I shoved the car into LOW gear and floored it. I expected the car to take off like a scalded cat but my faith and enthusiasm were quickly proved to be utterly misplaced and completely unfounded as it ground to a halt half way the hill. There was only one thing to do. Jim jumped out and, using all of his twenty years' service in the Police force, stopped the traffic behind us. In broken French, he then had to explain to the queue of vehicles that they would have to reverse so that I could also reverse and have a run at it!

Incredibly, they all dutifully obliged and with about twenty metres behind me and a clear road in front of me, I reversed up, Jim jumped back in and, with a Murray Walkeresque cry of "Go! Go! Go!" I hit the 'loud' peddle.

Every nut, bolt and seal on the engine screamed at us to stop as all six of us rocked backwards and forwards to try and help to get some momentum. The car made it up the first piece of shallow incline and the noise from the engine was relentless as it started to tackle the steeper slope. The car almost imploded, and there was a nauseating smell of burning clutch disc among other more noxious, and possibly human, odours emitted as we reached the apex of the hill where there was a sharp left turn. I dare not release the pressure on the accelerator as I took the left-handed corner virtually on two wheels. Outside, there were innocent men, women and children throwing themselves against shop fronts and people in the car itself being crushed against each other, this, alongside the accompanying soundtrack of whimpering, and claws hopelessly trying to get traction in the boot void as the dogs clamoured for some form of purchase until finally and eventually, the engine subsided and we reached the sanctity of the top of the hill.

There was a warm feeling on people's faces as well as in my undergarments as we realised the most traumatic part of the journey could well be at an end and it was at that point that, almost in recognition at what it had achieved, the back window went down and then up again, under its' own steam, to celebrate the event.

....

Never have six people and four dogs been as happy to be home as we were that day. We celebrated long into the night and made a pact that if we ever decided to make such a journey again, the clown car would stay in the barn.

It continued to serve our business with questionable distinction for some time. Fully adorned in magnetic door panels and an array of company information. You never quite knew how long it would take to get anywhere or indeed, if you would get there at all and, if you did arrive, how much of the car would be attached and intact; the exhaust fell off once and we casually stopped put it in the trailer and carried on like nothing had happened.

When, eventually, we sold the car – yes, someone ACTUALLY gave us real money for it! - I took the poor bast… sorry, potential buyer out for a test drive, making sure of course that I only turned left so that the four-wheel drive would disengage when required. The chap seemed *very* pleased with his new purchase. "Perfect" he said "for when I go out with my dogs"

That it was…providing of course you didn't want to go uphill and never, ever, tried to press the little red button with the Japanese writing.

Chapter 16 – How Hard Can It Be?
Removing a roof the easy way

Our house at Grand Villard stood on a plot of about 1 acre. At one point it had been a small cloth factory that made sacks and cloth coverings and there was still evidence of this if you looked in the row of barns that were opposite the main house. Over the course of time, the house had been extended as the factory got bigger and the various owners became slightly more affluent, but the barns remained pretty much as they were and were ideal for storage; in our case, car, van, boat, wood for heating and quite a lot of detritus that both we and the previous occupants had collected over the years. Indeed, there were a couple of barns that we never went into in the entire time we lived there, for no other reason other than we had no need to; slightly incurious you might think but true.

Some years previously, one of the earlier owners had erected an open-sided shelter made from corrugated metal sheeting which helped keep the weather away from the barn doors and openings and it was useful but, over the years, had become a bit of an eyesore.

The metal sheeting was arranged and overlapped so that when the wind blew, one end would lift up and then crash back down onto the panel below with an almighty crash that sounded like thunder.

The worry was that one day, the roof panels would dislodge, coming crashing down and either damage a paying guest's car or behead someone. To be honest, I was more worried about the former than the latter as if they were dead, they were unlikely to sue you, whereas a paying guest might object and might refuse to pay…which was a REAL concern! With that in mind we decided that to benefit the overall aesthetics and to avoid a catastrophe, we would remove the panels and the supporting frame. The frame itself was made from old oak beams which had seen better days and which could be cut up and added to our burgeoning pile of wood to burn in our wood burners during the winter.

Once the decision had been made and without further ado, I contacted the ever-reliable Jim who liked smashing things up and, rather too excitedly for a man of 40+ years, he arranged to come round a couple of days later.

He turned up with Yvette in tow. At first glance he was clearly over excited at the prospect of demolishing someone else's property. He was 'sweating up in the paddock' as we gathered the required tools and surveyed the job at hand. He adopted the role of 'Gold Commander' and strode over:

"The best way Wainio" he said "is to get up and take off the top layer of metal sheets then lift off the others once we've done that"

"...Good luck then" I replied "I'll be down here holding the ladder"

I was waiting for him to place 'POLICE CRIME SCENE – DO NOT CROSS' tape around the area to dissuade onlookers but this wasn't forthcoming.

As was his normal routine, he donned every conceivable piece of Health and Safety equipment; dust mask, gloves Hi-Viz jacket, hard hat, ear plugs.

I sat through a ten-minute presentation on how to climb a ladder – complete with Microsoft Powerpoint slides – and then, after being signed off as 'Site Safe' I was allowed to hold the bottom of the ladder.

He climbed up and, with crow bar in hand, started to lever up the nails holding the sheeting in place. Due to its' age and the fact that the nails had been left open to the elements for about 40 years, the head of each nail snapped off under the leverage of the crow bar. "Well, that's not working" said Jim after about 15 minutes of trying to get a nail out, "we need a new plan"

I suggested we simply lift up the sheets and twist them at the same time to tear the sheeting away and after doing this for about half an hour we had removed the sheeting and it lay in a pile to one side of the now fully exposed oak frame.

The frame itself looked very flimsy; flimsy enough for Jim to suggest that could save time by pulling it down using either my car or his – a Nissan X-Trail.

"I'll get your keys" I said, making the decision before he had the chance to argue. His little face was a picture as he thought about the job at hand and he started frothing at the mouth in excited anticipation.

He parked up about 20 metres to one side of the frame and from the boot of his car he produced a long tow rope, quickly tying the tow rope to the top of the frame and securing the other end to the tow hitch on his car. He was satisfied he was ready to go, and demanded we all step back to a safe distance; from where I was standing that meant going to Bournemouth.

He jumped into his car, started it up and reversed back a bit to give the rope a bit of slack then, with wheels spinning on the gravel, he launched the car forward.

Clearly the oak frame was a lot more secure than we had given it credit for. As the rope became taught, the forward momentum of the car was instantly halted and the back of the car launched up into the air about two metres before it came crashing down to the ground.

Pip, Jim's Labrador, jumped out the back of the car as it hit the ground and the door of the boot flew open. She quickly sought refuge at the far end of the garden where Yvette and Trudy had retreated to, and gave Yvette a tacit look that said everything required about the fiasco.

Jim leapt out the car to survey the damage to the frame, which was still standing as tall and as proud as previously…1-0 to the oak frame.

Several slightly more considered and a lot less 'gung-ho' attempts later, and having cut three-quarters of the way through the oak pillars with a saw, he did eventually manage to pull down the structure with the car whereupon it was chain sawed into small lengths and used as firewood for the following winter. Personally, I felt slightly uneasy; so, this is what it felt like to be blameless. It was an oddly unnerving experience; being able to blame someone else for a plan's abject failure, but somewhat comforting, and I got a warm fuzzy feeling knowing that nothing that had happened could be held against me in a court of law.

Jim decided that using his car as a 'weapon of mass destruction' probably wasn't the greatest idea he had ever had, an opinion forcibly reiterated by Yvette who suggested they have a debrief to discuss the afternoon's events and decide in what format the punishment should be administered; I smirked as I turned and whispered "...this is *definitely* going on your personnel file".

She then turned to Trudy and in a language in which they were both fluent, closed her eyes, shook her head and uttered, in a low, menacing voice through gritted teeth "...what a knob...".

Chapter 17 – Health and Safety: Oh Shit!

It is quite well documented that France has a bit of a 'laissez faire' attitude to health and safety; for example, there are no road markings on any of the exits or entrances to the main roundabout at the Champs D'Elysees in Paris, one of the busiest road junctions in France. I addition to this, drivers who are already *on* the roundabout are expected to give way to those wishing to enter the roundabout; with the predictably *hilarious* consequences as you can imagine! After all, French drivers are world renowned for being courteous and amenable – especially in Paris. On the whole, they tend to work on the basis that, as adults, you should be able to make your own mind up as to the best and safest way to negotiate a certain situation and, if it ends in your untimely demise? Well, you've only really got yourself to blame. Sometimes you get the feeling that people are going well above and beyond to find new and novel ways of killing themselves and exiting their own gene pool, but it's all taken in their stride and seen as a bit of a badge of honour and part of the 'fun' of getting the job done. Grown men get together to compare scars and gunshot wounds that are as a result of being part of the 'chasse', the French equivalent of a shooting party, and being shot by a fellow participant after a particularly long and boozy lunch.

The English, however, are far more subservient when it comes to rules; one need look no further than cricket as an example. Ten different ways to dismiss an opposition batter, five days in some cases to get a result and the bloody game *still* ends in a draw because of rules and regulations written in the mid-18th century by members of the then 'Star and Garter' club. I can't think of another game where the rules state that play can stop if the sun is shining too brightly to distract the player or players!

With that in mind, our own unwavering allegiance to health and safety laws sets us Brits apart. Fortunately, there was no-one looking when we 're-arranged' the main, timber joist of the barn in chapter 5 but, needing to remove a beam which was inconveniently positioned in one of our own barns and, having employed the services of Jim 'Trip Hazard' Hitch yet again, we were, once more, required to sit through the full 3-hour presentation and having finished the role play part of the safety assessment, we set to the task in hand.

After the great 'weapon of mass destruction' incident, Yvette decided to pull rank (she was a higher rank than Jim in the Police Force and no matter how hard he tried to deny it, we knew that she was always the hand that rocked the cradle…the influence peddler if you will)

Fully adorned in hard hat, security gloves, security trousers, ear defenders, goggles, 'I love Tommy Walsh' braces and an emergency tub of L'Occitaine hand cream, Jim approached the beam. I was holding one end, Trudy was holding the other and Yvette was in the middle.

Studiously, Jim started up the chain saw and, although almost unable to lift his arms due to the weight of the various safety devices he was wearing, he started to cut through the beam. His technique was sound and we knew he was really concentrating because he pursed his lips and looked like he was about to kiss a moose or plunge a blocked sink.

In hindsight, perhaps it should have been Yvette who was wearing the safety gear as the chainsaw made short work of the 200mm by 100mm joist. With a loud '*CRACK*' one half of the beam, being held in the wall at one end, dropped down and we heard Yvette's teeth chatter as it landed squarely on her head. Unfortunately, she'd been holding the other half as instructed by Jim.

"Well blige me" said Yvette "…what a rather unfortunate thing to happen…" or words to that effect anyway. They say that foul language shows a lack of linguistic knowledge. I would challenge that as there were words thrown about that day that hadn't been heard in polite society since Shakespeare was a boy; good word knowledge all round I'd say…

Having sewn his testicles back on, Jim decided it was time for a large gin and tonic - after all it was the afternoon somewhere in the world. The beam was cut, Jim was in trouble again and all was good with the world.

By this time, the Hitches were coming to the end of their 2-year work sabbatical and we had only one more job that they had agreed to help us with: tree cutting for one of our regular clients. Based on past experience, what could possibly go wrong.

Chapter 18 - The Gueret Rope Trick

When the big day arrived, Jim and Yvette arrived early. The house we were going to was further away than any other. It was in the Haute Vienne, our neighbouring department, near to Rochechouart, about 140 kms away from where we lived.

We loaded the car up with the bare essentials: red wine, bread, cheese, white wine, an appropriately sized charcuterie, rose wine...you get the picture and, with everyone on-board, dogs in the boot and trailer loaded, off we set.

The trip usually took about two hours and the tasks at hand included grass cutting on our newly acquired ride-on mower, lots of strimming – and I do mean lots – and tree cutting. Jim and I decided that we would tackle the manly tree cutting whilst Trudy and Yvette could do the girly stuff, which they took well as you can imagine.

About 125 kms into the journey and I had a sudden realisation that in my excitement at how much cheese we had, I'd forgotten to put the ladder on the trailer. This would have been fine had all of the trees that required pruning or lopping been about 6′ tall, however this was an issue – and a big one at that – as they were mature apple trees and pine trees. What we needed, was a plan.

When we arrived, we unloaded the equipment that I HAD remembered to bring and I sent Jim off to 'reccy' the outbuildings as I had previously seen a ladder in the barn. He came back carrying a very long, wooden ladder and asked me if this was the one I had seen.

"Yes! That's it" I replied "should do the job no problem". With that Jim put one hand upon one of the ladder uprights and the other hand on the other upright and, with minimal effort, the two came apart and the entire set of rungs fell, as one, to the floor. "Plan B then?" I enquired.

We hunted around and eventually found a single, four feet long, metal ladder. Not long enough for the work we had to do but we were sure that if we put our minds together we could make it work. Trudy started on the ride-on mower, Yvette was strimming like there was 'pas de demain' and Jim and I were throwing crab apples at each other and giggling.

"...if you two don't stop pissing about I'll bang both your bloody heads together!!" said Trudy "...it's Jim, he started it!" I said, pointing at him and bouncing a rock-hard crab apple off his forehead at the same time.

After being chastised and warned that any further behavioural infringements and we would have to answer to Yvette, we set to task and came up with a plan so beautiful in its' simplicity, it couldn't fail.

Our plan was for Jim to slowly climb the ladder and I would act as a 'brace' for the ladder, allowing Jim to climb up, virtually to the top whilst I held him upright. He could then reach up and cut the required branches from the overall height of about 10'. It was faultless and we couldn't really see a downside; it wasn't as if he was holding a newly sharpened chain saw or anything…oh hang on…

It's surprising how difficult it actually is to brace a ladder with a fully grown man standing on the top of it. Especially when he is waving a fully working chainsaw in the direction of your face. As the chainsaw, not for the first time, invaded my personal space I ducked and let go of the ladder. I didn't mean to…it was a reflex action. As I let go, I saw Jim walking across the grass whilst balanced precariously at the top of the ladder swaying like a cobra being charmed out of its' basket by a snake charmer's pungi. All I heard from the top of the ladder was "WHOAA…WHOAA!!" as the ladder fell to the ground, followed by Jim and the still revving chain saw. The plan needed tweaking. We tried it with me at the top of the ladder to no avail and even tried tying the top of the ladder to the branch we were cutting which, to no-one's surprise was the worst idea of them all. We did finally master the 'brace and balance' technique as it's now known in the trade and whilst it did work, I wouldn't go as far as saying it was as effective as a two-stage ladder.

After lunch, where much cheese and wine were consumed, Jim and I decided to tackle the more difficult branches up in the canopy of one of the trees.

I joined Jim about half way up the tree and, with me holding him in place in one hand and holding a branch out of the way with the other, we started dismembering the tree branches. To our astonishment, this method was working remarkably well, right up until Jim lined up a branch and before I had a chance to stop him, and with me only registering a barely audible "no!" he cut through the branch. At this point a much bigger branch which was being held back by its' smaller sibling and which had the tensile strength of a crossbow, whipped round and, with a rustling of leaves and a loud '*THWACK*!' hit Jim full in the face.

Not for the first time that day, Jim ended up flat on his back at the base of the tree with the remnants of the branches and me on top of him. The one saving grace was that as we were higher up, he had time to switch off the chainsaw before he landed.

With grass cut and trees almost pruned and lopped, we decided to abandon work for the day whilst Jim and I still had the requisite number of limbs. We finished off the food, drank the dregs from the wine glasses and set off for home. It was a long journey home, Jim and I giggling about the days' events, Trudy and Yvette casting disapproving eyes in our direction but we knew, deep down what they thought:

How on earth did we end up with such a couple of bellends?

Chapter 19 -The Return of the prodigal couple

For those who remember, 2012 was a bit of a momentous year. Events that happened included the cruise ship '*Costa Concordia*' sinking off of the coast of Italy after the ship's captain, allegedly, let his girlfriend 'have a go'. He then abandoned ship, leaving 300 passengers to their fate; of which 32 died. Vladimir Putin was elected President of Russia, Barack Obama became President of the USA for the second time, the UK hosted the summer Olympics, Chelsea won the UEFA Champions League final, beating Bayern Munich in the final in Munich...*that* went down well with the locals causing Poland to immediately reinforce its borders. Sweden won the Eurovision song contest and Lonesome George, the last known individual of the Pinta Island tortoise subspecies, died in Galápagos National Park, thus making the species extinct...shame. It was also the year when Trudy and I concluded that France had suffered enough and decided to go back to the UK.

As mentioned previously, Limousin Property Care had been very successful, but running a business in France is difficult - and very expensive. After a while, the joy of working for 3 days a week just to pay your business and 'social' charges wears a bit thin and so, with heavy heart which was counter-balanced by a much lighter wallet, we decided to come home.

Our home at Grand Villard had always seemed to be well received, so we were confident that it would sell; we just weren't sure how long it would take. My first objective was to find myself a job back in the UK; not the easiest of tasks when you lived there, but made even more difficult when you were 500 miles away! Interviews were clearly going to cause an issue but I set to task looking on various websites and contacting recruitment agencies, most of whom showed a distinct lack of interest once they found out where I was currently residing. After speaking to a number of so called 'experts', I came across a small, one 'man' (woman as it turned out) agency, run by a lady - Lucy - who had actually worked in my old industry - office products - and, having spoken to her in person, she was confident she could help. Because of the ineptitude and overall lethargy demonstrated by most of the recruitment companies I contacted, I decided to do it myself, and sent emails out to a number of Sales Directors with a view to then following this up a short time afterwards via telephone. This proved very successful and, after organising a trip back, I arranged three or four interviews over a three-day period. Lucy had also managed to secure me an interview with a company and so, full of enthusiasm, I set off a few days later to get myself a job. The journey home was by no means simple; it was mid-winter and flights from Limoges to Stansted were sparce; made even more 'sparcerer' by the fact that Limoges airport was gripped by winter ice and the only flights available were from Charles de Gaulle airport in Paris to Luton! I didn't mind getting up early to go to Paris but it seemed an inordinate amount of effort when your final destination was Luton! It was rubbing salt in the wound! We set off at 3.15 am to get the airport in time for the flight and made it with about 30 minutes to spare. Luckily the flight had been delayed due to the inclement conditions so the normal '2-hour check-in' window had been extended.

Day one was successful; interviews resulted in the usual "we've got other people to see / we'll let you know / you want to earn *HOW MUCH??!!* sort of response. Undeterred, I approached day two full of vim and no less amount of vigour. I had three interviews, one from Lucy and two I'd managed to secure through my own efforts. This was the day…it was going to be good…I could feel it in my water. My first interview was over in Enfield and was very positive and, again, the gentleman promised to get back to me after agreeing salary etc with his HR department; things were going well as I headed off for my second interview in Essex…Basildon to be precise…   Bas Vegas…Basilwood as it's known to the locals.

At the time, the UK was preparing to host the Summer Olympics and as part of these preparations, had erected a huge 'BASILDON' sign as you entered the town; like HOLLYWOOD only with more bird shit on it.

The interview went extremely well, they liked me, I liked them and, most importantly, they didn't bat an eyelid when I told them my salary expectations. Having been interviewed by the Managing Director, the plan was for me to try and see the Sales Director before I left the following morning to come back to France. The problem was that he lived in Lincolnshire and wasn't around. I was determined to get a job whilst in the UK. I wasn't leaving that green and pleasant land (actually it *was* Basildon so not very green and slightly unpleasant if truth be told) without securing a job. I had another appointment in Surrey later on in the afternoon and by the time I came out from the interview, I had about an hour to get there. I chased around the M25 and it was then that I had an epiphany.

I cleaned myself up after the epiphany so that it didn't stain the seats of the hire car, and phoned my previous interviewee asking if I could see the Sales Director that evening. A plan was hatched that he would drive down the A1 to the South Mimms services and I, similarly, would cancel my third appointment and drive completely around the M25 to the A1 and meet him there. It had better work. I still hadn't heard back from the first interview and was throwing all my eggs in one Basildon basket. I arrived at the allotted time and, armed with a large Starbucks cappuccino - reasonably priced I thought at only £175.00 – I awaited his arrival. He arrived, dressed in an immaculate suit, swarthy, olive-skinned complexion and blindingly white teeth that certainly had the SR 'ring of confidence' about them.

The interview was a roaring success. I said all the right things in all the right places, I was an absolute delight and he realised he couldn't possibly carry on without me…OK I made that bit up but it *did* go very well. I went 'all in' and chanced my arm. I told him that I had had another offer of a job - big fat lie - and that I wanted to make a decision before going back to France the following day. He said he would contact me as soon as possible to let me know the outcome.

I didn't get much sleep that night as I was continually thinking about the 'what ifs' should the result not be favourable. I was heading back to the airport about 7.30 am the following morning and was desperate to know the outcome. Waiting for people to contact me is definitely NOT something I do well, and found myself checking my phone every couple of minutes…had I missed a call? Had I accidentally put the phone on 'silent' mode?

I was due to board the plane at 9.15 and, by 8.55, I had used up every last drop of self-restraint and was absolutely on my last thread of nerves waiting for the call. 8.56…still no call, 9.00…nothing, then, at 9.06, the phone rang; It was him.

We exchanged pleasantries and I tried to sound as calm as I could. He apologised for keeping me waiting and then uttered the fateful words "…good news! We'd like to offer you the job!!…". I was both delighted and massively relieved and phoned Trudy to tell her the good news; Operation Blighty was on.

When I got back home, I gave Trudy a full de-brief of what had happened and we made plans for me to go back to the UK a few weeks later in preparation for my start date at my new company. We were going to start up an admin file called the 'HOME PREPARATION' file, but I feared the title may be truncated; and I didn't think 'PREPARATION H' was entirely appropriate. We had some loose ends to tie up in relation to Limousin Property Care, and the plan was that any work other than gardening would be distributed to our network of local artisans. Trudy was going to stop doing the bed and breakfast and concentrate on doing the remaining gardens. Of course, the one major, outstanding issue, was the selling of the house. We contacted a local agent and they advised us that they would be delighted to put the house on their books…bearing in mind they charge 30% commission (in France this is normally added to the sale price as it is paid by the purchaser) I have no doubt they were delighted!

A few weeks later, I flew back and took up residence at my sister's house near Rayleigh in Essex - about 10 minutes on a good day from Basildon.

Saying that, I suppose whether or not you think being 10 minutes from Basildon is a good thing is open to a certain amount of debate.

Regular telephone calls to Trudy advising her of how things were going back on 'civvy street' ensued. I got back into the swing of things and was charged with the responsibility of looking at potential houses for us to purchase. I can't lie; I was very uneasy with this newly acquired responsibility. I felt wholly unqualified to make such decisions bearing in mind my only previous involvement in this process was, as the reader will remember, purely ceremonial. To shoulder some of the burden…sorry…blame…, I enlisted the help of Trudy's sister, Tracey. I worked on the basis that, with her diplomatic nature in all things controversial, she may well prove to be slightly more objective when providing feedback on some of the houses Trudy wanted me/us to see; too far from shops, too close to schools, you get the picture. That seemed to be better than me saying "…just take my word for it love - it's a shithole!".

Meanwhile, back on mainline Europe, things were moving at a pace. The agent had shown the house to various interested parties and, lo and behold, we found ourselves a buyer. The relevant paperwork was signed and our need to find a suitable house in the UK became a higher priority. My need to go and look at 'potentials' became more acute and it became quite a slick procedure whereby Trudy would find houses, email the details to me, whereupon Tracey and I would then arrange visits with the relevant estate agent.

Houses came and went, none being of real interest. Trudy then found a house in Haynes near Bedford needing some renovation and so, remembering the fateful words that I had uttered upon leaving France *"…that's it! I'm done with DIY; if there's one thing I'm not buying, it's another renovation project…"*, we duly signed on the dotted line and bought another renovation project.

Once the purchasing process in both countries had been finalised, we set a suitable date for completion and I then set a date in the diary to hire a van and drive to France to collect our belongings. We had decided to drive back in convoy with me in the van and Trudy, plus Ben and Holly, in the car.

The big day arrived to collect the van. I left work at the appropriate time and headed off to pick up the van from a hire centre in St Albans. Leaving my car in the 'Arrivals' compound, I headed back to my sister's house at the wheel of my newly acquired 7.5 tonne lorry; the biggest my licence would allow. The return trip was around the M25 and, if nothing else, having a constant stream of other road users intent on committing suicide before your very eyes, does sharpen the focus and heighten your skills.

By the time I reached my sister's house I felt as though I'd been driving it for years and in full control. The following morning, I woke up, got dressed and was out the door by 5.30am. The previous night had been spent tossing and turning...it wasn't so much the turning but the tossing that kept me awake all night (steady everyone!)

I knocked on my sister's bedroom door and whispered "I'm off; thanks for everything...". "Zzzzz...drrvsafly..." she mumbled incoherently, and, with that, I was off.

I made my way down to Eurotunnel at Ashford, where I had been advised by the telephone operative that I needed to go to the 'Freight' section of the terminal. I did as instructed, and found myself surrounded by huge, articulated lorries on their way back to Europe. There was a multitude of different languages being spoken and arms being enthusiastically waved as the drivers leant out of their cabs to speak to each other and catch up on news. For the uninitiated amongst us, the process of loading a lorry onto the freight shuttle consists of driving your lorry forwards onto the open sided rail carriages, whereupon a car arrives and collects you to take you to a buffet car where beverages and dubious looking sandwiches are available...I know! Who knew!

Soon it was going to be my turn; talk about 'in at the deep end'. These guys were professionals and *they* were struggling!

The Rumanian lorry and driver in front of me edged forward and started his run onto the carriage. There was a terrible scraping noise and his wagon shook from side to side as he misjudged the entrance to the carriage and scraped the side of the wagon on the large metal poles that marked the entrance. There was an audible cheer from the other drivers and an array of gestures, some of which were made with an excessive amount of gusto, and most of which enlightened him and anyone else to his apparent well-known proclivity to manual, one-handed self-gratification.

He reversed (which meant that the eight lorries behind him ALSO had to reverse…including me) and embarked on his second run which, thankfully, he got right and he manoeuvred his lorry onto the carriage then disembarked to survey the damage; no amount of luke warm coffee or 3-day old cheese sandwiches were going to ease *his* suffering.

My embarkation was much less dramatic; notwithstanding the fact that my lorry was about a third of the size of his. Still, that didn't stop me setting the air brakes with a loud and very pleasing *'PSSSHHH '*, jumping down from the cab and giving him a look that said "THAT'S how you do it Pedro!!". He in turn gave me a look that said something entirely different.

I waited diligently for the taxi/car to collect me and after arriving at the buffet carriage, took my place, warm coffee in hand, next to a chap who was delivering milk. He told me that from the time of loading the milk into the wagon, he only had 24 hours to deliver it. "What happens if there's a delay?" I enquired. "They get cheese" he said. We laughed, and I helped him break the crusts off of a corned beef sandwich.

When we arrived at Calais, we made our way off of the train and I made my way to the motorway that would signal the start of my journey. I had the foresight of bringing with me my portable Satnav to help with the journey in case of issues. Trudy was the one who normally did the driving and to be honest, despite the fact that we had completed the journey quite a few times over the preceding 8 years, I was normally asleep by Calais so wasn't particularly 'au fait' with the precise directions.

I had taken the opportunity at Ashford to replenish my supplies before undertaking the main portion of the journey and so, armed with a six-pack of Yorkies and a family size bag of Werther's Originals (all civilised people agree that the Werther original toffee is the 'go to' sweet snack for those wishing to combine the pleasure of a chewy, succulent, caramel based confectionery item, with the jeopardy of never quite knowing if, at the end of the experience, they will retain all of their fillings). Having studied my *'HGV driving for idiots'* handbook and paid special attention to the section entitled *'everyday interaction with members of the public and other road users'*, I perfected my 'dropping tomato sauce down my vest' and 'leering' techniques, in accordance with the recommended guidelines. Satisfied that I had a working understanding of what was required, I quickly scrolled through my 'Collins French Dictionary' and reminded myself how to say *'Wahay! alright darlin' lovely tits!!'* in perfect French whilst waiting to disembark. I felt ready for the off.

My first point of reference was again Rouen. Some 2 hours south of Calais, this turned into 2½ hours when I realised that the lorry was fitted with a 50mph speed restrictor. I hadn't noticed when I picked it up due to the fact that I had been on the M25 and never got above 35mph or into 4th gear. The discovery of the speed restrictor meant that I had to do a quick recalculation of my journey time as the 430mile trip normally took around 7 hrs; an average speed of about 60mph. With the top speed of 50mph and, therefore, an *average* speed of about 40mph, the trip was likely to be extended to about 10½ hours! One thing was certain; I was going to need more confectionery.

A couple hours or there abouts later, I entered the outer peripheries of Rouen and started following my Satnav to navigate the town to get to the other side and back on the motorway. Being a man, I clearly knew the route better than the Satnav having slept for most of the previous journeys, so I summarily dismissed her instructions and ploughed on. Before long I was confronted by a height restriction barrier at the entrance to a tunnel, and a sign that said '*Camions Interdit*'…Lorries prohibited. I saw the height restriction barrier just prior to driving into it and managed to pull over into the adjacent lane - much to the surprise of the lady driving in the lane at the time - where there was a narrow street which took me around the lorry free zone. I couldn't understand why the Satnav had taken me along that route until I realised two things; 1) the satnav hadn't…I had and 2) that normally we were in a car and no restrictions applied whereas this time I was in a lorry. After a diversion of about 6kms I was back on the motorway and it was that point I slammed my foot to the floor, braced myself against the 'G' forces as the engine galloped its' way to 35mph…40…42…at this rate I'd be stopping for dinner before it reached 50mph!

Some 9 hrs later I throttled the engine back and came into land at Grand Villard. Trust me, when you have a long journey ahead, 50mph is very…very… slow. Still, I had arrived, unscathed, and, more importantly, so had the lorry. There had been quite a sizeable insurance surcharge to pay because I was taking the lorry out of the country so the last thing I wanted was to damage the lorry.

Trudy had spent copious days and weeks packing up our belongings and I can't lie; it had been really difficult for her. Villard had been her dream and we had spent some wonderful time there and had some incredible memories that we would remember for the rest of our lives. The neighbours leaving home grown veggies in a basket outside our front door when we first arrived; just to make us feel welcome. The annual 'voisinade' event where everyone in the village cooked a dish and met up in someone's garden and we all had a good ol' chinwag and a laugh.

Packing up to leave seemed sad. From a financial perspective we would be better off in the UK but we loved our French life and deep down we knew that we wanted to someday come back; albeit perhaps when we could have a bit more time for ourselves and get the work/play balance a bit more equal. Having packed everything up, we had a reasonable night's sleep and the following morning I set off straight after breakfast on the journey back. Trudy had to wait to give the keys over to the estate agent so followed on about an hour later. Having given me an hour's head start, she caught me up and went past me pretty much prior to me getting on the motorway, and we arranged by telephone to meet up at the services for refreshments. This continued to be the theme for the remainder of the trip; me setting off in the lorry, pushing my foot through the floor in order to eek another one or two miles per hour from the shrieking engine, and Trudy flying past me, waving, about 20 minutes later. We had arranged to stay the night in Calais before getting back on the Eurotunnel the following morning and it came as no surprise to me that Trudy arrived at the hotel about 45 minutes before I limped into the car park; by which time, Trudy was sitting outside at a table with a large gin and tonic.

Once again, focus, care and diligence were the 'buzz' words as I reversed the lorry into its allotted space.

212

"Don't hit anything – just don't hit anything" I said to myself as I manoeuvred backwards. There was a tremendous sense of relief as finally I applied the handbrake - '*PSSSHHH*' - (Ed. I know… it's childish; but I just like making the noise as I write it!) and jumped down from the cab, the early evening sun glinting majestically off of the avalanche of Werther's Original wrappers and silver foil from the Yorkie bars that followed me out as I dismounted. All the while I was reversing the lorry and sweating from my rectum, Trudy watched on, glass in hand. Having finished her gin and tonic, she asked me how the journey had been and took great delight in reminding me how long she had been there awaiting my arrival. I reminded her that I was hamstrung by a vehicle that had arthritis, and could she excuse me as I felt a bit queasy after devouring more caramel and 'E' numbers than any human had previously attempted or indeed achieved, and needed to avail myself of the facilities.

Crisis averted…just…We nipped out for something to eat and retired to our suite; a room so small that it was impossible to be in it AND have your luggage with you. The bathroom was a pre-fabricated plastic shell that had a shower cubicle, toilet and sink all cold-pressed out of one sheet of plastic! Ingenious in theory but the efficiency of which was questionable in practice. Admittedly you could brush your teeth at the sink whilst washing your legs in the shower but, also, when using the shower, the soaking of the toilet paper was inevitable.

Fortunately, we realised this and removed the roll of paper before it was too late. Had we left it until the following morning, I fear the impaired structural integrity of the paper would have become apparent at a more critical juncture.

Having breakfasted on a piece of cardboard as it was a more filling and viable alternative to a croissant, we set off for the Eurotunnel terminal where I, again, would be required to use the freight section. We arranged to meet on the other side and this was achieved as planned whereupon we headed off to the new house. As before, Trudy went off as an advanced party as we had arranged to meet her sister and boyfriend Baxter - (see chapter 2) - at the house to help us unload. After what seemed like days, I *finally* fought my way around the M25, up the A1 and arrived at my destination; our new house.

As I approached the house, I could see Trudy, Tracey and Baxter outside waiting for me to arrive. I could also see that parking outside the house was not an option; the road was narrow and the van would block at least one half of the street to traffic. I decided to turn round so carried on another 100 yards until I saw the entrance to the village hall. I was relieved beyond words that I made two trips around the M25, driven up and down the M20, loaded the lorry onto the freight carriage at Eurotunnel, both in the UK AND in Calais, driven about 1100 miles in total and I was finally back. With the air of a man with a completed mission under his slightly expanded belt, I reversed the lorry into the entrance of the village hall…and watched as the brick pier on one side of the entrance tore an 18″ gash in the fibreglass side of the lorry before falling serenely to the floor…so close…and yet…Having heard the gut-wrenching noise, Trudy, Tracey and Baxter came to survey the damage. "…Oh dear…" said Baxter, "…bollocks…" I replied. Before long we were joined in looking at the remains of the brick entrance by one of the village locals who happened to be the warden and who also had the keys to the hall. "…good afternoon…" I said, trying to put a brave front on the recent events, "I'm Mark, this is my wife, Trudy… we've just moved in to number 34…you wouldn't happen to know a builder, would you my good man?"

We were back, and it was just like we had never been away.

Epilogue:

There were many other stories and tales like the ones regaled above. All of them contributing to the rich tapestry that was our life in France.

Jim and Yvette had moved back to the UK in 2012, not too far from where we eventually ended up living. Returning to the UK was, as it transpired, a very timely thing to do. Shortly after arriving back in the UK, I sadly lost my dad. The one saving grace was that as much as both he and my mum loved coming out to see us in France, we were back with them when he passed away.

The 'Hitches' still have the same house in France and Trudy and I were back in the UK until 2018 when we decided to return to France before the UK left the EU. We are here now, and the adventures continue to carry on. The Crêped Crusader rides again...but that's for another time.

Acknowledgements:

When I first mentioned the idea of writing down some of the tales and adventures we encountered and endured as owners of our Chambre d'hotes, it was Trudy who gave me the confidence to actually put pen to paper (well, fingers to keyboard if we're honest) and for that I will always be grateful. Without her as my safety net, I may not have completed the job. As hard as it seemed at the start, actually, I loved every minute of the process and found myself laughing as I recalled some of the stories. I would also like to thank my many friends who encouraged me and continually asked me when it would be finished...I know I said it would be done AGES ago but I lied. Anyway, it's done now – so buy a copy! I'd like to thank Cathy Pace for all of her input and help with the copy-editing on the original stories and for laughing in all the right places. Thanks also to Will Healy for his amazing artistic help on the cover.

I would also like to thank my family who, after reading the first draft, surprisingly, said they thought it wasn't bad, and say sorry to my two beautiful dogs, Holly and Phoebe - I'll try to make up for all the missed walks with treats and biscuits...I feel certain that will be deemed acceptable.   Not forgetting, of course, my first dog and best friend, Ben. A piece of you will always be with me.

Mostly, I would like to say thank you to EVERYONE who came to stay with us at Grand Villard in the chambre d'hotes; without you there would be no stories, and to *you*, dear reader, for actually buying a copy of my book; you've made a middle-aged man very happy. I hope you find every tale, at the very least, humorous but, if only one story makes you smile well, that's one smile you didn't have before you read it.

Printed by Amazon Italia Logistica S.r.l.
Torrazza Piemonte (TO), Italy

31910598R00123